IT BEGINS
WITH A DREAM

IT BEGINS
WITH A DREAM

Peter Legge
with
Duncan Holmes

EAGLET PUBLISHING

Eaglet Publishing
4th Floor, 4180 Lougheed Highway
Burnaby, British Columbia, V5C 6A7 Canada

Canadian Cataloguing in Publication Data

Legge, Peter, 1942-
    It Begins With a Dream

Includes index.
    1. Success.   2. Self-actualization (Psychology).
I. Holmes, Duncan.   II. Title.
BF637.S8L455 1996   158'.1   C96-910089-2

ISBN 1-55056-425-0

First Printing   March 1996
Second Printing   August 1996
Third Printing   January 1998
Fourth Printing   July 1998

Jacket design by Mark Kamachi
Typeset by Debbie Craig, Sheila Lloyd, Mack Morrison
Edited by Robin Roberts
Printed and bound in Canada by Friesen Printers

Other books by the Author

How to Soar With the Eagles

You Can If You Believe You Can

*Dedicated to the
memory of my mother
Winnifred Ivy Legge
1917 – 1994*

CONTENTS

Dedication

You might think, in the great scheme of things, it would have been much tidier for parent-child love and affection to have been automatically included in the human package.

It wasn't, of course. Nowhere does it say that kids have to get along with their parents or parents with their kids. We come into this world inheriting all kinds of patterns from those who came before us, but, despite some similarities, we are all clearly individuals who choose our loves with considerable care. Parents get lumped in with everyone else.

If we learn to love our parents, if they become friends and confidants, it is not because it was destined to be, it's because we work at it.

Throughout our lives, we often end up getting along with, or being influenced by, one parent more than the other. I won't presume to understand why girls may get along better with their fathers or boys with their mothers. But these things happen. We form bonds that, inexplicably, are stronger one way or the other.

While those in my business and social circles may believe my father has contributed mostly to the shape of my life and the careers within it, I would quickly say no. It was my mother who played the bigger part, who influenced my life's directions, who challenged, supported, pushed and occasionally shoved me into the best directions.

That doesn't make my dad anything less than the great guy he is. I've written elsewhere about my father and *his* incredible life achievements. I've worked with him for many years and admired his ability to set and achieve goals, to always remain the gentleman he is and to beneficially influence those around him. Nevertheless, my mother was the one who contributed the most to the things I have done.

I speak in the past tense because my mother died on August 2, 1994. She was 77 years old. She had not been well, but her passing was unexpected. I learned of her death after being paged at an airport somewhere in the U.S. Midwest.

We can never know when calls of this kind will come, and no matter how well we think we might handle this kind of news, it is invariably shattering. Suddenly someone you love is no more. Suddenly everything becomes only memories. Spoken and written words may remain along with the photographs and personal possessions, but there is no more *person.*

I flew home that day filled with sadness. I cried without shame. I remembered so much. Because I could never again speak to my mother, I decided in my own awkward way that I would write her a letter. Who knows why we do these things; it doesn't matter. If there is comfort in our actions, so be it.

I wrote to my dear, blessed mother and she took the letter with her into the world where she had gone. I wrote these words:

I never told you enough times how much I loved, admired and respected you.

You were a truly wonderful mother.

Since you gave birth to me, you have never doubted me – you have always loved me and encouraged me in everything I ever did. I'm sure many times you must have wondered how I would turn out, but you never, ever gave up on me. Much of what I wanted to accomplish in life was because I wanted you to be proud of your son.

Through your illness, I blame myself for not giving you enough attention and perhaps helping you live longer. Forgive me for this mum, please forgive me. You seldom complained about anything, even in your struggle.

My prayer is that you didn't suffer. My prayer is that you were proud of me, that you knew I loved you beyond words.

Nothing I have ever experienced could have prepared me for this awful pain of your death. As I write this I can't understand how it will be without you. You will be missed so very much. Our family was so important. Thank you for loving Kay, Samantha, Rebecca and Amanda. You have touched our lives forever.

I pray today as I look upon your face that you are with Jesus and you are healed and well and looking forward to seeing all of us in a few years when we will be together and laugh and love again.

My heart is broken. No son could have had a more wonderful mum. God blessed me with the very best he had.

Good-bye my dear mum. I will always miss you. I will never forget you and I will see you again.

Your devoted son,

Peter

Rest in Peace

August 5, 1994

It was a joy to write the first two books in this series. *How to Soar With the Eagles* is now in its fifth printing and has recently been published in England. My second book, *You Can if You Believe You Can*, is now in its fourth printing and sales continue to climb. I never cease to be amazed at the feedback from readers telling me their lives have been touched by my stories, that they have been guided into more positive directions.

My mother had similar influence on *my* life. For all of her love and good works, I dedicate this new book to her and the rich memories that will always remain.

Peter Legge
Vancouver, B.C., Canada
April 1996

CHAPTER 1

Savouring Sweet Victory

SOON AFTER THE END of the Second World War, my parents decided to send me to a private school for boys in East Sussex. The school was in a little town called Heathfield, halfway between what is now Royal Tunbridge Wells to the north and the seaside town of Brighton to the south. (Some knowledgeable Brits might also say that it's just down the road from Butcher's Cross and Five Ashes. I just *love* the names of England's towns and villages.)

I was enrolled at a private school because my parents felt it would afford me more subsequent opportunities than if I were to attend a regular school in London. I don't know why that is, but the belief persists.

It was a big and brave decision for my mother and father. Both were working and the fees they would have to pay would mean huge sacrifices for both of them. But it was one of the first big dreams they had for me. I would begin the next stage of my life with quality education, coupled with the kind of discipline that is traditionally part and parcel of the highly regulated private school system.

When the train left London's Victoria Station in the winter of 1947, I was just five years old and we were puffing southward into the first big adventure of my young life. I had absolutely no idea what lay before me at Tavistock Hall Preparatory School for Boys in tiny Heathfield. I was an unknown quantity heading into an unpredictable future.

School uniforms were pretty standard at schools in post-war England and even today they haven't changed much. Uniformity, I suppose, is part of the process. We wore short grey pants, knee socks, grey shirt, striped tie, maroon blazer and maroon school cap, complete with the school crest. Sharp outfit, but certainly not showy.

With me on the train that morning were other London kids who were headed to the same destination. We sat together for the 90-minute journey and, at the age of five, that 90-minute train trip could well have been a journey halfway around the world.

I could write another book about my schoolboy adventures at Tavistock Hall, but for the purpose of this volume, I will tell just one story.

The event happened in my final year, not long before the Legge family left England for Canada. My parents had decided that Canada, and specifically Vancouver, British Columbia, presented infinitely more opportunities for success than did post-war

Britain. They were big dreamers and, at age 12, I would be part of their dream.

The summer before we left, the annual Tavistock Sports Day was about to take place. Full of vim, vinegar and Olympian dreams, I tried out for every event on the card. But the event in which I really wanted to excel was the Half Mile for Boys. It was the glamour event, the premier race of the day. Four times around the track, the winner invariably ended up being a school hero with adulation of the highest order and at *least* 15 minutes of fame.

After the time trials, they had a field of 15 – and I hadn't made the cut. I was disappointed, but what the heck, there were other events and I would still have the chance to depart from Tavistock Hall in style.

But it was not to be. Other forces were at work and things would change.

Part of the routine at Tavistock Hall required parents to donate trophies for specific Sports Day events. Private schools do a great job getting kids started, but like every other school in the world, they always have a need for funds for just about everything. My parents had sent a trophy for, you guessed it, the Boys Half Mile for 12 year olds and, as you already know, I wasn't, at this stage, in the race!

Enter the head master.

There were 250 of us, all in school uniform, seated for breakfast when he arrived to deliver the news. As always happened when the "head" arrived, the hubbub ceased in an instant. Not a whisper above the sea of porridge bowls.

He fixed me with a stare.

"Legge," he said. "You were too slow to be one of the runners in the half mile, but your parents have donated a trophy. I guess I'll have to put you in the race."

It was a good-news, bad-news story. Incredible motivation for a 12-year-old boy!

So Sports Day came and there I was at the starting line, the 16th runner in a newly augmented field. The gun went off and we ran.

At the end of the first lap, I was dead last, exactly where I should have been. Then, as I passed the clubhouse turn, I caught the eyes of my mother, father and grandmother and knew that being last in the 1954 Legge Classic would not be good enough for the kid who bore the proud Legge name.

I put my 12-year-old butt – or the English equivalent of the expression – in gear and began to reach out. Bigger steps. Faster steps. An injection of adrenalin to get me going.

At the end of the second lap I was in 10th place and the family group had now moved to the front of their seats and were cheering me on. At the end of the third lap, I was running fifth and victory seemed entirely possible. My family was standing and cheering wildly.

I won that race. The field dropped away behind me as I plunged victorious into the tape.

How *did* I win that glorious day all those years ago? I don't know exactly how I did it, but I think that encouragement counted for a lot and, somewhere along the way, self-confidence contributed something as I strove for an attainable goal. Even the headmaster, in his strange way, was throwing out a challenge. I would show *him* that No. 16 could be No. 1.

I still have the little trophy my mother presented to me on that very special day. There's an old photo of us in this book, me in my cricket whites when I stepped up to receive it.

Races aren't always exhausting physical endeavours. They can be as simple as setting a goal that you think may be just beyond your reach, and going for it. You'll be surprised how many times you can take home the prize. It can be big money, power, whatever. It can be as simple as a moment's satisfaction.

I have dreamed many dreams since that day at Tavistock Hall. Some of my dreams – *many* of my dreams – have come true. And I have always found that races are won lap by solid lap.

I urge you to be there at the starting line for *your* race, to give it your best every step of the way, to savour sweet victory when the race is done.

We are such stuff as dreams are made on

—The Tempest, Act IV, Scene I
William Shakespeare

CHAPTER 2

Life Is A Selling Job

I TEND TO GRAVITATE TOWARD people whose ideas I respect. Invariably, they keep coming up with new ideas from which I can learn. Did someone say, "from which I can *steal*?" Maybe that, too, but in most cases I think people are delighted when you tell them you introduced one of their good ideas into your life and it *worked*. It's like these books. If they are useful to you, I figure I've made a worthwhile contribution; and you got your money's worth.

Those of us who spend a lot of our time on the motivational speaking circuit share each other's ideas. If someone writes a book, we all buy it. If we are able to catch a presentation at a conference, we make notes and recycle the good stories. It's global chit chat and we all know that anecdotes and good ideas are tools of our trade.

I've talked often about motivational speaker-trainer Zig Ziglar, one of the giants of the business. Zig always has something to add to the wealth of information he gives regularly to his audiences. It was Zig who said: "People don't care how much you know – until they know how much you care about *them.*"

Ain't it the truth? How often have you been in a conversation with someone and all they've done is go on and on about what a spectacular life they've led? They've *been* everywhere, *done* everything and collected a drawer full of T-shirts to prove it. You just know that when they've finished unloading all this on you they'll wander off into the crowd and tell someone else exactly the same things.

How much more welcoming is the person who, after a moment of introduction, looks you right in the eye and says: "So, you look like an interesting person. Tell me about the exciting things you've been doing lately."

"Wow," you say to yourself, "this is different. I've been asked a question and I think this person actually wants to listen to my answer." You can feel that something good is happening, that the moment is really worthwhile.

You've likely encountered the same situation in business. Your company says it has an open-door policy all the way to the president's office. If you have a problem, says the policy, you can take it all the way to the top. But, more often than not, it just feels like you're annoying the people who have promised to listen to you. Your supervisor, the first person in the line, is terrified you will get past him or her. So you're derailed two minutes into the conversation. There is no real interest in what you have to say; your supervisor would much rather spend the energy covering a very nervous backside.

Remember trying to buy that new car? You spent all that time telling the salesperson exactly what you wanted and he mumbled, "Uh huh, uh huh, uh huh," as you spoke and you just knew he wasn't listening. And at the end of it, as though aroused from a deep sleep, he said: "Interesting, but I don't really think it's what you need."

Not what I need?! I've spent two years researching the vehicle I just described to you and it's *exactly* what I need.

Give the guy full marks for trying, but not for *listening,* not for giving you credit for the work you have done, for the program you have outlined so well.

A better reaction would surely have been: "I think we have exactly what you're looking for. Let's go see." He'll have plenty of opportunity later on to sell you the air conditioning, the super sound, the power rear vision mirrors and the leather covered options.

As Zig Ziglar says, let people know you *care* about them.

"I have this idea."

"Tell me about it."

"I'm worried about my kids."

"Let's talk about it."

"I've got a big decision to make."

"Fill me in on the details."

"I don't know whether or not I can handle it."

"Tell me about your problem and maybe we can work it out together."

Idealistic? I don't think so. It's always easier when the load is shared. How many times have you said to someone: "I really *do* wish you had let me know. We could have shared the load and made it much easier."

Sacrifice, no matter how small, can solve problems and bring huge rewards.

Zig Ziglar tells a sharing, caring story about sacrifice that he had read in a newspaper (I told you we all recycle each other's stuff!).

The incident took place back in 1910 when blood transfusions and other medical miracles were not as common as they are today. Jimmy, a 10 year old, was devoted to his six-year-old sister, who had fallen from her bike and cut an artery in her leg. Bleeding profusely, she was fading fast by the time the doctor arrived at the children's home.

The doctor clamped the severed ends of the artery, but her heart was already failing. In desperation, the doctor turned to Jimmy and said: "Son, will you give your blood to help save your sister's life?"

Jimmy swallowed hard. "Yes," he said, "I'll do it."

In minutes, Jimmy, lying on the kitchen table, felt his blood flow directly into his sister's veins. For 30 minutes the doctor and the family watched anxiously and prayerfully and, in time, Jimmy's sister began to improve. Relieved, the doctor turned to Jimmy, who was trembling like a leaf.

"What's the matter Jimmy?"

"Wh . . . when do I die?"

The doctor frowned, then suddenly realized that Jimmy had misunderstood his request. What the boy heard was that the doctor needed *all* of his blood. He had hesitated briefly, but he was quite ready to give everything – including his own life – to save his sister.

We give, we listen, we understand who our customers are – in business, in family, no matter where the sale is to be made. Life is a selling job. Whether we succeed or fail often depends on how well we motivate and respond to the people who come and go in our lives.

We must listen with open hearts and open minds. We must understand that people we deal with are often moving in a direction that may be completely different from the one we believe is right. But we must listen. We must try to achieve the win-win goal.

Unfortunately, we often take people for granted. We fail to make an active and continuous effort to do and say the things that will bring them *our* way, that will create trust, that will encourage teamwork, that will motivate them to a higher plateau of achievement.

Again and again I see individuals and organizations performing to the smallest potential of success or failing entirely because they simply don't listen, don't try to understand, don't try to make it happen *together,* because they neglect the human element in business and life. We should never be too busy to listen, because by listening, we learn.

People don't care how much you know – until they know how much you care about *them.*

Nice words, Zig. For my money, words to live by.

CHAPTER 3

The Diamonds of Tomorrow

EVERY MONDAY SINCE AUGUST 8, 1989, I have circulated a memorandum called *Insight* to the management and staff of Canada Wide Magazines and Communications Ltd., the company of which I am CEO, president and publisher.

Each *Insight* is just one page long – we're all much too busy for more – and is a Legge view of the world that comes from my own observations or from any of hundreds of other sources that inspired me between editions.

I'm amazed *Insight* has endured. Like New Year's resolutions, *Insight* was an idea that might well have died on the vine. But miraculously it kept going and I know that its readership and influence extends well beyond the Canada Wide family that really *is* Canada wide. For all I know, it may have ended up on office desks and suspended by refrigerator magnets around the world. I *told* you I dream big dreams – and I have a rich imagination!

In the *Insight* issue of May 29, 1995, I recalled a favourite Legge theme and headlined the page with a quote from the incredible motivator Brian Tracy that read: "If you want to earn more, you must learn more."

I then went on to say that the No. 1 growth industry in North America is education, continuing education, gathering more knowledge in our chosen field, growing and learning. I reminded my readers that Charlie "Tremendous" Jones, a formidable motivational speaker and trainer, had said that we will be the same people today in five years, except for the places we visit, the people we meet and the books we read. Ain't it the truth?

I asked the Canada Wide team: "Where will *you* be in five, 10, 15 years? How are you preparing yourself for a future that's always coming your way? Why is it important to *learn* more and *grow* more and why *now*?"

I told them a story that went something like this:

One night a group of nomads were preparing to retire for the evening when suddenly they were surrounded by a great light. They instinctively knew they were in the presence of a celestial being and with great anticipation, they awaited a heavenly message of great importance that they knew must be especially for them.

Finally a voice spoke through the light: "Gather as many pebbles as you can," said the voice. "Put them in your saddle bags. Travel a day's journey and tomorrow night when you stop to rest, count your pebbles and you will be both glad and sad."

"Hmmm," said the nomads. "The first time in our lives we're

stopped in our tracks by a great light, the first time in our lives we're pumped for a revelation that will set us on the road to fame and fortune and what happens? We're told to gather pebbles! Get a life!" Or some other, more suitable nomad-type words.

But gather pebbles they did. Said the nomads: "When there's a bright light and a big Charlton Heston voice, you never know."

But it was a token gathering at best. A few pebbles in the saddle bags, a night's sleep and another day's journey. They expected little.

The next night, remembering the glad and sad message of the night before, each reached into his saddle bag. Surprise! What had yesterday been pebbles, today were diamonds. Giant, sparkling diamonds of great value.

Glad? They were ecstatic. Sad? Yep. Opportunity had knocked and they didn't have the confidence or the trust in themselves or their benefactor to answer the door. The celestial being would not be back.

It's not unlike the parable of the talents in the New Testament. Jesus told of a nobleman who was going abroad and before departing he gave each of his servants five talents – an amount of money – telling them to trade with it until he returned.

When he came back, he asked each for a report. The first had built his pot from five to 50 talents.

"Great," said the nobleman. "You are an excellent servant and because you have proven yourself worthy in a trifle, you are now head honcho in 10 of my towns."

The second servant said: "Your five has made 25, sir!"

"Great," said the nobleman. "You get five towns."

The third servant said: "Here are your talents, sir. I kept them safe in a napkin because I was afraid of you. You are a hard man, picking up what you never put down and reaping what you never sowed."

"You rascal of a servant," said the nobleman. "I will convict you by what you have said yourself. You knew I was a hard man, picking up what I never put down and reaping what I never sowed! At the very least you could have deposited my money into the bank so that I could have got it with interest when I came back."

And the nobleman took the five talents that the third servant had kept in the napkin and gave it to the man who had made 50.

"To everyone who has, shall more be given," said the nobleman. "From him who has nothing, even what he has shall be taken away."

We all have an opportunity to capitalize on what we've been given. To do less is to shortchange ourselves. Use it, or lose it, as the saying goes.

Too often, we're inclined to sit back and complain that others are making it and we aren't. Mostly it's for the very simple reason that others are capitalizing on opportunity, filling their saddle bags today for their needs and wants of tomorrow. They're not keeping their talents wrapped in napkins, but are exploiting them to the full in the brightest of social and economic spotlights.

Nike's challenge to the world of would-be athletes is to: "Just do it!" Tie up your laces and start running. Compete against others if you must, but regardless of the competition, go at the very least for a personal best.

Shakespeare said: "Be not afraid of greatness; some are born great, some achieve greatness, and some have greatness thrust upon them."

That's what happened to the servant who maximized his investment challenge and made 50 talents from five. Because he did well with a "trifle," he ended up with an empire of 10 towns. Greatness was thrust upon him and I don't doubt at all that he did well.

Too often we believe we'll never be able to handle the rewards that may come when we stretch our talents to new dimensions. Try it some time. You won't believe how satisfying and rewarding it can be to succeed.

So often I've told my audiences that the greatest problems in business, no matter how bad they may appear to be, are invariably disguised as opportunities.

"We appear to have a problem here."

"Let's see how we can fix it. Let's get a whole lot of great minds together and let's fix it!" Remember Apollo 13? Fixing the unfixable.

I read that 92 per cent, *92 per cent,* of the things we worry about never happen. Think about it. Remember all those nights you lay awake worrying about tomorrow's likely tragedies, those endless scenarios of *what ifs*? Almost none of them happened. Right?

We owe it to ourselves to tap into the personal resources each of us has, to be braver, to work our way more often to the head of the line, to speak up in the crowd, to give it when we're asked for an opinion.

The opportunities don't often come with bright celestial light and big booming voices, but I can assure you there's no time like the present to start picking up pebbles. Lots of pebbles.

They are, without a doubt, the diamonds of tomorrow.

CHAPTER 4

A King-Sized Effort

I HAVE FOUND THAT, along with the unbeatable service they provide in getting us from one place to another, airplanes are great
places for reading.

In my opinion, reading beats working with computers. A lot
of people trot out computer "notebooks" on planes these days. On
night flights I have often seen pools of light from row after row of
people who insist on continuing their work up there in the sky. It
all seems a bit intense. But I digress . . .

In the early summer of 1994, I was flying back to the coast
from Toronto and, being a reader and not a notebooker, I picked
up a copy of *Time* magazine and became engrossed in a story
about what had just happened and was continuing to happen in
the distant and mysterious African country of Rwanda.

A writer called Nancy Gibbs, with input from a number of

correspondents, began her story with these words:

"There are no devils left in Hell," the missionary said. "They are all in Rwanda." Actually, they brought Hell with them; you have only to watch the rivers for proof. Normally in this season, when the rains come to these lush valleys, the rivers swell with a rich red soil. They are more swollen than ever this year.

First come the corpses of men and older boys, slain trying to protect their sisters and mothers. Then come the women and girls, flushed out from their hiding places and cut down. Last are the babies, who may bear no wounds: they are tossed alive into the water, to drown on their way downstream. The bodies, or pieces of them, glide by for half an hour or so, the time it takes to wipe out a community, carry the victims to the banks and dump them in. Then the water runs clear for awhile, until men and older boys drift into view again, then women, then babies, reuniting in the shallows as the river becomes the grave.

Aid workers have guessed that anywhere from 100,000 to 500,000 Rwandans have died since the civil war between the Hutu and the Tutsi reignited a month ago. But no one knows how many – and we may never know. The bodies not rotting by the roads are buried in mass graves or floating down the rivers, far away from the arithmetic of history. With this latest tragedy in its long litany of tribal massacres, Rwanda joins Angola, Sri Lanka, Liberia, Bosnia and Nagorno-Karabakh in defining what barbarism means in the late 20th century, and defying the rest of the world to try to do something about it.

I read on.

Unless led by a hated tyrant, a country that loses its head of state by violence often goes a bit mad. In Rwanda the madness was spreading even before the night of April 6, when the plane carrying President Juvenal Habyarimana and his neighboring head of state Cyprien Ntaryamira from Burundi was shot out of the sky over the capital of Kigali, plunging into the gardens of the presidential palace. Habyarimana was a Hutu who had grabbed power in a coup in 1973 and worked hard to hang onto it. He was on his way back from a peace conference in Tanzania that was meant to end years of struggle between the minority Tutsi and the ruling Hutu. Instead, with his death, the fighting turned into massacre after massacre after massacre.

The Hutu instantly blamed the Tutsi rebels of the Rwandan Patriotic Front for the death of their President. Within minutes after the crash, soldiers of the presidential guard, who most resisted any sharing of power, took to the streets along with mobs of drunken young men and began hunting down Tutsi civilians, killing them where they stood. Western nations quickly whisked their nationals to safety, leaving terrified Rwandans to fend for themselves. As the tales of murder began to filter out, it became clear that there were no sanctuaries: blood flowed down the aisles of churches where many sought refuge; five priests and 12 women hiding out in a Jesuit center were slaughtered. A Red Cross ambulance was stopped at a checkpoint, the six wounded patients dragged out and bayoneted to death. Toddlers lay sliced in half, and mothers with babies strapped to their backs sprawled dead on the streets of Kigali. The fighting was hand to hand, inti-

mate and unspeakable, a kind of bloodlust that left those who
managed to escape it hollow eyed and mute . . .

When confronted by talk and words of overwhelming tragedy, I think that each one of us reacts in a very personal way. But there are also many similarities in the way we feel.

Senseless, I said to myself. Absolutely bloody senseless. I finished the *Time* story, leaned on my fisted hand and looked out the window beyond my weary, reflected face into the night sky.

Like you, I have written cheques for any number of charities. Like you, I believe that as well as ridding us of a bit of guilt and helping to uncork some of the milk of our human kindness that each of us has within us, writing a cheque serves a practical purpose. It helps to pay the bills, furthers whatever the cause, helps to get at the root of whatever the problem. We all do it, and after reading the *Time* story on the plane that night, I was determined to write a cheque to help the Red Cross help anyone who needed it in bloody Rwanda.

By the time the plane had landed, I felt that while a cheque might be good, it wouldn't be good *enough*. If I could somehow widen the circle of involvement in response to this tragedy, the benefits to those who needed them could be infinitely larger than anything I could do with one cheque.

A stone thrown into the pond? A light from one small candle? Reach out and touch someone? The metaphors ran wild, and so did my determination and imagination.

When I got home, I told my often-surprised wife that I was going to do something for Rwanda. I told her I had read about it on the plane, that the story had disturbed me, that no matter who was right or wrong out there, human beings were suffering and they needed help. Would she help? Would she support my worthwhile, but probably zany, idea? Of course she would. You need all the help you can get to make dreams come true.

It was June. In September, with some hard work, I figured we could hold a benefit lunch and raise as much money as possible for the Red Cross in Rwanda.

Once again, to get things going, we rallied the troops at Canada Wide Magazines and Communications Ltd., the company of which I am president and in which I share ownership. They've been rallied before and as a first line of offence for a cause, they always come through. Their enthusiasm sent an appealing wave through the community and in 90 or so days it was they who motivated others and closed our ticket sales.

But I needed more focus. I found it in a fax that had landed on my desk almost as I was landing from the trip to Toronto. It came from the exiled king of Rwanda, then living in Washington, D.C. He was seeking help for the Rwandan cause and I was on his list.

A light bulb went on! We could invite the king of Rwanda to lunch; add to our knowledge, help the cause. I called him, offered him a plane ticket and, perhaps not surprisingly, he said yes. Someone else for the dream team.

Costs for the event were to be kept to a minimum. An elaborate meal was out of the question with a cause of such gravity. Soup, a sandwich, no beer or wine. Vancouver's Westin Bayshore gave us a superb break on the food and we twisted other arms to make sure the "proceeds" of the event would be maximized.

We ran a four-page insert in many of our magazines, telling the Rwandan story to our half-million subscribers and other readers, publicizing the occasion in every way possible. The Canadian Red Cross was on board. We had dovetailed into *their* dream.

The publicity caught the attention of Vancouver public relations guru Ray Torresan. Ray told me that a client had read about what we were doing and wanted to pick up the entire tab for the lunch!

And it all happened. His Majesty King Kigeli V was our special guest. He spoke in French and my daughter Rebecca, who is bilingual, translated. His words clearly came from the heart.

At the end of the day, together with the lunch proceeds and additional donations that rolled in, we presented $180,000 to the Canadian Red Cross Society, a cheque I could never have written on my own, money that was generated because a dream was shared.

I don't feel like any kind of hero because of what happened. I just felt that on this occasion, I had to do more than attempt to carry it alone.

Rwanda and our world will continue to unfold in sometimes beastly and sometimes beautiful ways. As they do, each of us has the choice to light a candle to help someone find the way.

CHAPTER 5

Back to Capistrano

THERE'S NO DOUBT ABOUT IT, we humans have achieved a lot since the world began. And many of the things we have done have been most commendable – a tribute to the smarts that come with the human package.

That's the good news. The bad news is that, while we've been doing many things that we believe are for the betterment of all of us, it has often been a selfish process. Too often we have waged wars, turned away from suffering, done far too much damage to the earth, wrongly believing that our planet will serve us forever as a resource for everything we may ever need.

The good news once again is that, in the nick of time, we seem to be realizing that some massive attitudinal corrections are in order. We can't keep waging wars and turning away from those in need. We *must* learn to live in closer harmony with the animal, vegetable and mineral resources that make planet earth the attractive, life-sustaining place it is.

I could be wrong, but I think many more of us have become conscious of the fact that this sharing and giving has to happen if we're to look forward to a continuing, better world tomorrow.

I also think many of us are beginning to realize that the value of this planet can be counted in many more ways than those we might consider as simply economic. We're stopping more often to not only smell the roses, but to consider the lilies of the field and how they grow, to learn lessons from the beasts of the forests, the birds of the air. The wonders of the natural world are inspiring more of us to take stock, to think anew about life, our dreams and our personal and social responsibilities.

On several occasions, I have driven down Interstate 5 in Southern California and every time I get close to San Juan Capistrano, I think about the swallows. I've never been there on March 19, but apparently on that date every year the swallows come winging back, regular as clockwork, from their winter home in Argentina, to spend the summer in and around the Mission San Juan Capistrano.

For those of us who fly the international air routes with any regularity and appreciate the great distances, the migratory achievements of birds seem even more miraculous as we gaze from the windows of aircraft than they do from reading about them or studying their routes on maps. It's almost unbelievable that it actually happens – and with such regularity.

The story of the journey of the Capistrano swallows is as fascinating as any in the world of our feathered friends. They fly 12,000 round-trip miles from California to Argentina, most of them over water. That's a lot of flapping!

Unlike a 747, swallows can't make the trip south or north without a break. So how do they do it? While it sounds incredible, I'm told that the swallow carries with it in its beak a small twig. When the bird gets tired, the twig becomes the "boat" on which it rests before resuming its journey. Really.

I have no idea whether or not this is an urban or an ornithological legend, but I like to believe it because anytime anyone or anything has a dream or a goal of great dimension, I can find inspiration for my *own* dreams.

I'm delighted to think that a swallow finds Argentina a great place to spend the winter, and that it can make its way north to California and arrive on exactly the same date each year for the summer. Credit the body clocks of birds, but credit too the courage and stamina of a swallow that knows where it's going and gives everything it's got to get there.

The natural world has thousands of similar stories that demonstrate the realization of big dreams.

On February 13, 1971, I was working as a standup comedian at The Cave Theatre Restaurant in Vancouver, B.C., the opening act for the Mills Brothers, three of the world's greatest pop vocalists. I was honoured to be part of the bill and I hope they would say the same about me!

It was a Saturday night and between the two shows, twin brothers Peter and Jeffrey Barnett, famous in Vancouver as founder-operators of the Pizza Patio restaurant chain, and later of the Elephant & Castle restaurants, as well as for their good works with Variety International, showed up at the dressing room. They had a proposal. After the second show, the Barnetts asked, would we like to head on over to the city's Queen Elizabeth Theatre to participate in the Variety Club Telethon?

Back then, telethons were a relatively new concept. Fund-raisers were just beginning to learn of the power of television, how it was possible to commit people hour after hour to a worthy cause, to entertain audiences and raise money at the same time. I had never been involved with Variety or the telethon that Peter Barnett was producing, but we agreed to be a part of it.

For whatever reason, something clicked that night and it was to mark the beginning of my Variety International life. I per-formed then and, for almost all of the subsequent years, I have been a co-host of the telethon, a master of ceremonies at countless Variety events, and the chairman of a program called Cash for Kids that has raised nearly $5 million for Variety. Along with such luminaries as Roger Moore, Dame Vera Lynn and the indomitable Bea Arthur, I am an International Variety Ambassador .

In the summer of 1995, I was honoured with the Variety Heart Award, recognizing what was, for me, a true labour of love – the privilege to work in ways where I can be effective for less-advantaged kids.

In my response at the Heart Awards Dinner, I reminded the audience that the dream of Variety simply says: "We intend to help them all."

I told the story of the swallows of Capistrano and talked about dreaming big dreams. I also told a story that took place in the aftermath of the 1988 Armenian earthquake that killed more than 55,000 people.

In the midst of the devastation, a father left his wife at home and rushed to his son's school, only to discover that the building had been flattened by the earthquake. After his initial shock, the father remembered the promise he had made to his son: "No matter what, I'll always be there for you."

His eyes filled with tears as he surveyed the pile of rubble that had been his son's school, but the promise remained strong. "No matter what, I'll always be there for you." He remembered the walks to school, the building's pattern, the location of what had been the classroom. He began to dig.

Others said: "It's too late; they're all dead; you can't help; there's nothing you can do; you'll make things worse; go home."

To each, the father said: "Are you going to help me?"

When firefighters tried to pull him away with warnings of possible explosions, he said only: "Are you going to help me?"

When the police came and told him he was angry and distraught, he said: "Are you going to help me?"

He dug alone for eight, 12, 24, 36 hours. And in the 38th hour, he lifted a boulder and heard his son's voice.

"Armand," he shouted. "Is that you?"

"It's me, Dad. I told the other kids that if you were alive you'd save me; and that if you saved me, you would also save them. I told them about your promise, that no matter what, you would always be there for me. And you were, Dad, you were!"

"Are you O.K.?"

"There are 14 of us left out of 33. We're scared, hungry and thirsty, but we're alive."

"Come on out, son."

"No, Dad, let the others come first. I know I'll be O.K. You are here. You kept your promise."

I have learned in my Variety Club years that British Columbia's special needs kids will keep asking: "Are you going to help me?" And with enormous commitment, Variety will keep saying: "We intend to help them all."

It has been a privilege to be part of Variety's great work.

Fifty years from now it won't matter a bit what kind of a car I drove, what kind of a house I lived in, how much money I had in the bank or what kind of clothes I wore. I just hope that the world will be a little better because I was able to help a child. That's real satisfaction.

The swallows of Capistrano carry a twig to help get them to their destination. It's self-help and it's in their genes to do it. For some humans, it's more difficult. Some of us are unable to lift the twig or even to find it. The opportunity for the rest of us is to enter into a life in need and offer to help.

It's one way to a better world.

CHAPTER 6

A Bookshop in Bethlehem

A PUBLICATION THAT PROVIDES INFORMATION to public speakers asked me to jot down some ideas about why I think writing books like this, making tapes and creating brochures are important adjuncts to my public speaking career. I began by telling a story.

Two years ago, during a visit to Bethlehem, my wife and I walked into a small store called The Three Arches. Nothing too special about it, except that there in that little retail outlet, in that city thousands of miles from our home in Vancouver, were copies of my first book, *How to Soar With the Eagles*.

I'm sure the world's best-selling writers take this kind of thing in stride. Wherever they go, their works are displayed, translated into every imaginable language. But for me, new to the game and always interested in self-promotion, my encounter with an *Eagle* in Bethlehem was indeed a thrill. Not only did the moment give me a lift, but it also made me realize that I had made a good and important decision to back up my career as a public speaker with the publication of that first book and the others that would follow.

It wasn't a new idea. Motivational speakers, movie stars, sports heroes, politicians good and bad all seem to produce a book or two at one time or another. Books, the written word, no matter how elaborate or imperfect the presentation may be, become part of the record.

As a motivational speaker, I've had the privilege to hear many of the giants of my profession. Their words and the way they delivered them have inspired my own career. But while their presentations were powerful, I quickly discovered that what I learned from them was never confined to what they said on the stage. Inevitably, there was much more information in the books they had written and the tapes they had recorded.

I concluded that it's not enough just to be able to speak well and deliver a consistently strong message. To consolidate your career and really serve the diversified needs of your audiences, you need to back up your work with quality products.

To me, the No. 1 reason for developing books and tapes that extend your message beyond the podium is *credibility*. Look around at any major speaking engagement and check out the learning aids and other materials available. You will quickly discover that the speakers who took their message from the stage and committed it to the page demonstrate a real commitment to the ideals they share in their presentations.

These products serve a secondary purpose. The impact of even the most powerful speech fades over time. But backed by a book or an audio or video tape, that same speech is kept alive. By replaying or rereading, the magic of the message can be relived at any time in the future. Need a lift? Start reading the book or listening to the tape, and you're back again, the messages reinforced.

Another important reason for developing products is that a demand exists for these tools. People who come to hear speakers like me are searching for knowledge, insight and information. They can listen, leave and hope to retain something of the message. Books, audio and video tapes offer them a chance to take the message home for further study. And, of course, I won't deny that it's an extra sale for me. Why not? If people are prepared to pay for knowledge, I'm quite prepared to enjoy the benefits of the sale.

People like souvenirs. On a vacation to Hawaii, we not only take pictures, but we might bring back a T-shirt. At a Rolling Stones concert, we'll pay a fortune for a CD, jacket or book that will help preserve the memory of it. We humans treasure important and special times with things we can touch, read, hear, even smell. I have friends whose homes are awash with the scent of lavender oil brought back from a holiday in Provénce.

Looking at product development from a business perspective, books, audio tapes and other materials can serve a speaker in two important ways. First, they provide an excellent vehicle for self-promotion. Whether or not you're there in person, your products continue to deliver your message. They permit you to reach beyond conferences, through specialty shops and book stores – as far away as Bethlehem!

Second, with careful planning and preparation, these products are an excellent way to generate additional revenue.

For the most part, I've found it doesn't take much persuasion to convince most speakers of the need to support their work with informational products. Many have to overcome a more frightening hurdle. "Where," they ask "do I get my ideas?"

You will find, as I did, that the answer to *that* creative dilemma is actually quite simple. Let your personal experiences be your guide to the presentations you create. Draw on the wisdom of others by all means, but be generous with stories, anecdotes and insights from your *own* life. Use them in your presentations, and use them again when they become your books or your tapes.

By writing about the things you discuss in your presentation, you give people an opportunity to take home the things they found meaningful in your speech. It will cost them, but it will be counted among their prized possessions.

Are there additional words of wisdom in all of this? I believe that no matter what we do in life, there are always "add-on" opportunities to make whatever it is we're doing bigger and better.

Read any book about successful selling and you will find that those who succeed get close, very close, to their existing customers and prospective customers. Sales may be made, but customers are *kept* with tender, loving, consistent contact. I produce books and tapes for that very purpose. They are tools to keep the Legge name up front in the minds of those who *have* heard me speak, and those who *may* hear me speak in the future.

If I talk to someone of influence on a plane, I follow up with a book, a business card and an order form. Similar opportunities exist for you to attract and keep customers, no matter what your vocation.

I'm fascinated by what the Saturn car company is doing to keep its customers, how its going all out to prove it will never take a customer for granted. For instance, the company invited all Saturn owners across the country to a drive-in movie to see *Apollo 13*. Not only did Saturn pick up the tab for the movie, but it kicked in $15 per car to pay for munchies at the snack bar. I'm willing to bet that gesture will play big indeed when Saturn owners think about their next car. It's not that a movie and popcorn is any big-dollar deal, it's the fact they *did* it. When is the last time *your* car company picked up the tab for a movie, for *anything?*

Yes, there has been great value in adding books, tapes and other products as adjuncts to my speaking career.

What are you doing for yours?

—◆—

Today's business leader
cannot justify his existence
by profit statements alone.

He must also render
service to his local, national
and world community

— Dorothy Shaver

CHAPTER 7

Everything Counts

A CONSISTENT THEME IN THE mixed bag of messages I present to audiences everywhere is that, in life, absolutely everything counts. I talk a great deal about action and reaction, about reaping what we sow. When computers first began to show their large, grey forms in our offices, we learned about GIGO – Garbage In, Garbage Out. Another bit of wisdom that might be added to the bag.

We are shaped by our surroundings. Education, reading, our partners, our workmates – everything we see and do contributes to the evolving creatures we are. Socrates observed that for every cause there is at least one effect. It is simple, beautiful wisdom. Everything counts.

If we wish, we can go passively through life. We can let the influences of the world wash around us. We can, if we want, be unaware that we're part of *anything*. You've met people like this. You can talk to them about all kinds of frivolous things, but try to take the conversation to a richer plane and you hit a dead end.

"I don't watch the news . . . don't read newspapers," they will say. "There's enough misery in this world without me having to know about it."

"Vote? No, I never vote. No matter what happens in an election, the same bad actors always get back in."

"Give to a worthy cause? Charity begins at home."

"Go back to school? For what? There are kids on the street with three degrees and they *still* can't get a job."

I find people who think in these terms are tremendously draining on the rest of us. If only they would realize that taking other directions in life can offer such wonderfully fulfilling rewards. I've suggested to my audiences that they look upon themselves as products or services that are for sale.

"We all know about features and benefits," I tell them. "Today I want you to rate, on a scale of 10, *your* salable attributes. You get along with people? You get along exceptionally well with people? Give yourself a 10. You follow up with tasks like correspondence automatically and effectively? Give yourself a 10. You're pretty good at finding prospects that may become sales? Give yourself an eight, maybe a nine."

We proceed through a list of the kind of attributes that we all believe are essential to a well-rounded personality, that may well contribute to our success. But along the way, we discover that in some (many?) areas, all of us are found wanting. If we're honest

– and why wouldn't we be? – we all find that threes and fours start popping up in this exercise of self-analysis. Broadening our knowledge. We score a four. Contributing to the enrichment of family life. Three. Staying healthy. Two. And so on.

If we don't conduct this kind of inventory from time to time, we discover much too soon that others are passing us by, that we get sick more often than we used to, that we have to walk away from important discussions about topics that should be part of our knowledge inventory. It's a horrible thought, but we're beginning to resemble those people at the top of the chapter we said we abhor.

Life *is* difficult. Life *is* complex. We *do* need some rules to live by, to keep up with, to play its many challenging games. I have often said that a convoy of ships can only move as quickly as the slowest ship. When all the ships are up to speed, the whole convoy starts to fly! It's the same in your business life, in your company. Deadweight slows everything down and other corporate and individual "convoys" start leaving you behind. Garbage in, garbage out.

In about 30 years of doing business, I have learned that you can function far better when you're working to a plan, when you can tap into the kind of secrets that, when practised regularly, can be catalysts for success. They are secrets born of common sense. They are part of every successful person's program.

Because this is your book and you bought it as a tool for learning, I would like to pass on my own secrets of success. Don't dismiss them because they might seem obvious or because you may have heard them before. This time, think about what they *mean* and how each can be injected into *your* program. Read them now and re-read them three months from now. Do a personal assessment inventory now and another one in the not-too-distant future. Determine if and how you have changed some of the ways you do things. If you set yourself a short-term goal, have you reached it? If you said you would investigate a career change, what have you done to move in that direction?

You don't have to answer to anyone but yourself, but what better person to ask the questions? You can't lie to that face in the mirror. "This, above all, to thine own *self* be true." Everything counts.

CHAPTER 8

Dream Big Dreams

EACH OF US, IF WE'RE LUCKY, lives for about 4,420 weeks. I've always thought that, in those terms, it sounds like a lot less than 85 years. If you're planning to live life to the full and stretch yourself into all of its inviting corners, you have to hustle. You have to dream big dreams *and live them.*

How many times have you discovered you *can* achieve what you set out to do? Remember how nervous you were going into that seemingly impossible challenge? The halting steps? *Moi?* you said to yourself. Yep, *you.* And you *did* it. You went in there and you slayed the dragon. Did you say to yourself: "Hey, that wasn't so difficult, what's next?" Or did you settle back again into your comfortable niche and praise yourself for the next 250 weeks?

Every millionaire or billionaire I've ever talked to tells me very early in the conversation that the biggest secret of his or her success is to dream big dreams, to plan long term. These people didn't get where they are by taking the cheap seats at the back of the bus. They said: "I'm heading for the top of the mountain!" And they began to chart a course that would get them there.

Microsoft billionaire Bill Gates, a man we all watch and listen to with great interest, says his success in business has largely been the result of his ability to focus on long-term goals and ignore short-term distractions. He continues to dream big dreams about developments within his own industry and he creates the kind of systems – with people and technology – that can make them happen.

"When change is inevitable," says Mr. Gates, "you must spot it, embrace it and find ways to make it work for you." That's the quote of a dreamer who dreams big dreams. You just *know* that if Bill Gates continues to head up Microsoft, the company will continue to serve and astound us.

It can be intimidating to read of Gates-type success. You might be saying to yourself that he was the right person at the right time, that he got the breaks, that no one will ever again succeed like he has succeeded. When comparing bank accounts, that may well be. But while Mr. Gates may have a special niche in the business world, there is also a special niche for *you*.

When I talk of dreaming, I'm not talking about *daydreaming*. Dreaming also means *doing*. You dream your big dream and you start to make it come true. You write it down, share it with a close friend, with your husband or wife, you begin to plot your course, breathe some life into it, keep fanning the flames that will make it burn brighter. Everything counts.

I have dreamed big dreams and many of them have come true. And I keep dreaming, reaching out a little more, taking calculated risks, believing that if I've climbed to all of these levels, I can certainly climb to some more.

We humans thrive on achievement, but the best of us push today's achievement quickly into history and move on to tomorrow's new goal. That's the fun of it. And who knows? It could even be the Great Purpose.

Vancouver billionaire Jimmy Pattison once told me that those men and women who dream big dreams have the capacity to achieve big dreams.

Jim Carrey was a stand-up comic playing the comedy club circuit in North America who dreamed of international stardom. Following his acclaimed success in the movies *Ace Ventura: Pet Detective*, *The Mask* and *Batman Forever*, he was interviewed on a Barbara Walters television special. He talked about his struggle to make it at the beginning of his career, the long, lonely nights on the road, and how six or seven years previous he had written a cheque to himself for $10 million and dated it October 1995. He kept this huge dream in his wallet, looking at it every day. Last year, Jim Carrey signed a contract to star in the sequels to *The Mask* and *Ace Ventura* for, you guessed it, $10 million – each. (And this doesn't even top his estimated $20 million paycheque for *Cable Guy*!)

Coincidence, fate, luck – or the realization of a bigger dream that he studied every single day for many years?

"You become what you think about most of the time." It is a thought that has been attributed to many people. I remember it coming from the late, great motivator Earl Nightingale.

Ralph Waldo Emerson, who spoke and wrote with eloquence about almost everything, said: "If the single man plant himself indomitably on his instincts, and there abide, the huge world will come round to him."

I interpret that to mean that while it may take time and while we may have to struggle to find what we're looking for, we become what we think about all day long. In any hunt for treasure, it helps to have a map, the keys to the doors, the secrets.

You can begin right now with Secret No. 1: Identify your big dream. Dream it. Do it.

CHAPTER 9

Do What You Love to Do

"DREAM BIG DREAMS" IS NO. 1 on the Legge List of Success Secrets. No. 2, and one of my favourites, is *"Do What You Love to Do!"* I added the exclamation mark because it's advice that needs to be *shouted!*

How many times have you met people who, in answer to the question, "If you had your druthers, what would you *really* like to be doing?" said, "Certainly not what I'm doing now." So why, I ask, are you doing what you're doing now? Security blanket? Fear of failure? In a rut? Laziness? Lack of ambition? What? Surely it can't be because you're afraid of potential happiness, contentment, personal satisfaction and a life fulfilled?

Just because you begin your career in one field doesn't mean you can't change and do something else along the way. If you have a hobby that absolutely turns you on, maybe there's a way to turn your hobby into a money-making career. I know of a couple who were in completely unrelated fields but they shared a love of birds. So they opened a store that sold everything to do with birds – backyard feeders, seed, tapes of bird songs, pictures, calendars, you name it. And the customers – and there are thousands of people out there who also love birds – *flocked* to the store (pun intended). The business took wings, so to speak, and, at last count, the couple have three stores and are loving every minute of their new careers. Sure it took courage and sure it took specific knowledge, but what tremendous rewards were in it for them when they began to do what they loved to do!

There's a remark attributed to a poor guy who's getting on in years. When he's asked, "If you had a chance to do it all over, what would you have done differently?" he replies, "I would have spent less time at the office."

If you keep struggling in an environment that just doesn't match your talents or your dreams, it's like parting your hair on the wrong side. It just won't work. You'll be frustrated, you'll be mean and nasty because you'll always find a reason to find something wrong with your job, with the people around you.

Get out of it! Get out of it *now!*

Break away from the routine that has had you chained for all of those years. No matter who you are, how old you are, how much you have socked away in the company pension fund, go out and do something you love to do. Feel the joy of waking up in the morning and realizing that at last you're being honest with yourself, you're no longer battling to discover a life *style,* that you've started to live *life* and you're living it *your* way.

Be kind to your family when you make your move. Tell them you're sorry, but that's the way it is. "A man's gotta do what a man's gotta do." "A woman's gotta do what a woman's gotta do."

Remarkably, you won't be damned by those around you. You'll be supported. "Good on ya, Harry," they will say. "I wish *I* had the guts to do what you're doing." And you will smile a big, silly smile and feel hundreds of tons of old, tired baggage suddenly being lifted from your shoulders. You'll hold your head a little higher. And while the immediate future may be tremendously uncertain, you will walk into it knowing that it's *your* future to make, that you're doing what *you* want to do.

The past is history
The future is a mystery
Today is a gift
. . . That's why they call
it the present
— Unknown

CHAPTER 10

Unleash Your Power

SECRET NO. 3: *Focus on Your Own Unique Talents.* It sounds simple enough, doesn't it, but all of us struggle with the problem of identifying what we do best and sometimes it can take a lifetime. We listen carefully when people say: "Wow, that's a remarkable talent you have. You could make a million."

"Yeah, but –"

"Yeah, but what?"

Too often we push our talents into the background and plod along with stuff we know is mundane and which, in every way, is unrewarding. Our talents, no matter how small and insignificant they may appear to be, need to be brought up front, touched up, explored and exploited.

"You do the most amazing things with your hands."

"Really? I love to work with my hands. Never get the time."

"Quite honestly, this is the best meal I have ever tasted."

"Really? I think I like to cook more than just about anything else."

"You made this yourself?"

"Yep. If I could muster up some bucks, I'd make a whole lot more."

"Your writing moved me to tears."

"I'm flattered. It's just a hobby."

So what are you doing about it? There are reputable firms that conduct tests to help you unearth your talents, hidden or otherwise. Often, their findings are quite amazing and you'll be offered a whole cartload of opportunity.

Your friends, family and associates can also be helpful if you're struggling. Ask them, "What do you perceive that I do well?" They will tell you, honestly. Maybe their input can be merged with what you discover from other professional consultants and one may confirm the findings of the other.

The important point in all of this is that you can make your search for success easier when you unleash the power of your special talents and take this power to its attainable zenith. To do it any other way means you're not being fair to yourself; you're hiding your light under a bushel, you're depriving others of the benefits of your brilliance.

Don't tell me you don't have it because I just won't believe you. We all have it. Each of us is gifted with a special something. All we have to do is begin pushing the buttons that will turn things on. Focus on your own unique talents and take my word for it: your life will begin to change in new and positive ways.

It isn't a coincidence that success and sacrifice share the same first letter.

*It is one of the most beautiful
compensations of this life
that no man can sincerely try to help
another without helping himself.*
—Ralph Waldo Emerson

CHAPTER 11

Imagine Yourself as President

AN ASSOCIATE ON THE SPEAKING CIRCUIT told me that, no matter how magnificent a speaker I might be, as a motivator, as an all-around, indescribably good-looking guy, two per cent of the audience will think I'm a jerk.

Wow, I said, that's not much fun.

Forget about it, he said, it's a fact of life. I couldn't forget about it. *Two per cent of your audience will form an immediate opinion about you and for your entire presentation, they will think you're a total jerk!*

Convinced he was right, I went into my next engagement with considerable interest. As I looked out at a sea of 1,000 eager people, I realized 20 of them were already mortal enemies. I spared them the embarrassment of asking them to raise their hands. But, hey, 98 per cent were on side. Not a bad way to begin.

I'm the boss at Canada Wide Magazines & Communications Ltd., a publishing company based in Vancouver, British Columbia. Our stable of fine publications totals 19 and we employ 105 people. Annual sales, give or take, are about $20 million.

I suspect that, as with the above-mentioned audiences, two per cent of the people at the office *also* think I'm a jerk. Maybe more! I do my best in my role at Canada Wide, but it's not a perfect world. Again, two per cent ain't bad.

Sometimes, no matter how hard we try in the business world, things don't work out. People quite happily contribute to the success of a company, but some of them just don't like the boss and that's the way it is. I respect all of the people at Canada Wide. I try to treat everyone the same and I'm mighty grateful for what they're doing for the company and, I hope, for themselves. The two per cent? It's a constant that in the scheme of things is quite acceptable.

While it is sometimes lonely at the top, it is certainly a position that can also provide incredible satisfaction. You get to make big decisions at the top, decisions that not only have a direct effect on the corporation, but on all of the people who serve it.

If I wake up one night worried about the future of one of our magazines, what happens the following day can have a far-reaching effect on a great number of people. If we sell the magazine, those people could be out of a job. That might be the bad news. The good news could be that a competing magazine is struggling, giving us an opportunity to move in and acquire all kinds of new business. That can mean more people will be hired, new offices will be opened, and so on. It's power, no doubt about it, and power, when you have it, can certainly give a lift to your life.

All of that leads me to introduce Secret No. 4 on the Legge List: *Imagine Yourself as Self-Employed. Imagine Yourself as President.*

In the very different world of two or three generations ago, we were mostly trained to work for others. Our minds and attitudes were that those of us who didn't choose the so-called professions would all end up being the servants of someone else, working stiffs on the production line.

"Whatcha gonna do when you grow up, Billy?"

"Work for Ford."

"Who ya gonna work for when you grow up, Sally?"

"Woolworth's."

They are the extremes, but it was rare that we thought of ourselves as future entrepreneurs – self-employed, the presidents of our own companies. And because we *didn't* think this way, I believe that we set ourselves up to be kicked around for the rest of our working lives.

"I've got 16 years, four months and 22 days before I retire. I tell ya, I can't *wait.*" You must have heard it. And the day the poor guy retires, he dies of a heart attack.

I'm not suggesting we all suddenly quit and become presidents. What I'm saying is that if we begin to *think* like presidents, like *owners of our own companies* where responsibility about decision making is paramount, then we begin to change the way we do things. We begin to plan better. We begin to look more globally at the way we do everyday things. We meet deadlines and cover the bases. We have more awareness of the things that need to be done, right now and down the road. We are more conscious of the people who come in and out of our lives. We don't start running around hiring and firing people, but we are more careful about who we entrust to do the things that need doing. We no longer let people "sell" us, take advantage of us, rip us off.

A business may require three competitive quotes on a job and a purchase order to get it started. Maybe we can do the same thing when looking for a new insurance company or making any major purchase. Presidents demand respect and professionalism. Why shouldn't you demand the same kind of respect?

Presidents prepare short- and long-term budgets. With all the input they can muster, they have a pretty good idea how things will end up a year from now. If *this* happens here and *this* happens here, *this* will happen here. Ideally, there are no surprises at the end of the year; progress has been made according to – or better than – the plan, and everyone is happy. It works just as well for individuals.

You can be a "president" in your own corporate work circle or as part of your team. Many companies are recognizing the benefits of doing exactly that – empowering people at every level to succeed; giving them the authority to take whatever it is they are doing over the top, and benefitting as they do it. Read anything Tom Peters researched and wrote. It is most rewarding.

And, if you like, you really *can* become the self-employed president of your own company. It happened to me. After working for years for others, I saw a publishing opportunity and I went for it. Overnight, it was my responsibility – but it was also my break. That was 20 years ago and I've never regretted what I did.

Maybe your own unique talents can lead you into self-employment. Maybe that almost-complete, better mousetrap you're building in the garage can be the beginning of something great, where the idea is exploited as it should be and the results of all your brilliance come right back to *you*. And if it's what you're looking for, you'll have the wealth you always wanted, with enough left over for your kids' expensive education!

There's nothing wrong with working for a corporation or a boss. My point in this secret is that you can do it a little different-ly. There's no doubt at all that the way you do things will be noticed. And who knows, your presidential approach may put you on a direct path to the *real* presidency. It's within your grasp.

Think like a president. Believe it's yours.

And never forget: When you arrive at the top, two per cent of the people will think you're a total jerk. Hey, I never said you'd get it all.

All of us are born for a reason,
but all of us don't
discover why. Success in life has
nothing to do with what
you gain in life or accomplish
for yourself.
It's what you do for others.
—Danny Thomas

CHAPTER 12

Where Are You Going?

IN ONE WAY OR ANOTHER, most of us keep some kind of a record of the things we have to do. At any business meeting, you'll see people pulling out their Daytimers or versions thereof to record all kinds of things: what they believe is important information gleaned from the meeting, the date of the next meeting, other business and social events, commitments that are important to their jobs and families: Get a haircut. Milk on the way home. Just kidding.

Computers have made all this record-keeping a lot easier. There are any number of software programs available to help us keep track of our lives, to remind us what we have to do today, tomorrow and weeks, months or even years into the future. You'll find that, as you get a bit older, you'll need such reminders much more often.

On any given day, you can find people wandering around parking lots completely lost. Was it 3B or 4B where I parked the car? The next time, they will make a note of where they parked the car and they'll go right to it.

There's nothing wrong or unusual about writing down important things. As a matter of fact, I count it as No. 5 on my list of secrets: *Develop a clear sense of direction. Write it down. Be specific.*

If you consider it important to be able to find your car in the parking lot, how much more important it is to note what you plan to do with your life.

A friend of mine recently told me that five years from now she and her husband will own a bed and breakfast/cooking school in the south of France. She wrote that promise to herself on a piece of paper and affixed it with a magnet to her refrigerator. I have no doubt that five years from now, the planned business will be open and thriving. It will happen because she wants it to happen, and every day she will be reminded of her attainable goal.

Sometimes I think we neglect to write things down because we don't believe we'll end up doing what we *say* we'll be doing. That should never stop us. Just putting it down on paper can often jump start a new era in our lives and, by achieving even the smallest goal, we may go on to something bigger.

So what *do* we write down? You could write down that you plan to win the lottery but, while it may be an easy first choice, it's hardly something we can control. Your list is one that should include short- and long-term goals that *can* be reached if you put your heart, mind and energy behind what you're planning to do. They can be a mixture of things that involve your career and your family. More often than not, the two are inseparable anyway.

Cover off the essentials. Do you have a will? This is much easier to do right now than it will be in some unexpected emergency in the future. Adequate insurance to cover what you want to be covered? How about your investment program? If you believe in yourself, investments at the earliest possible age can provide a measure of security for the life you want to lead with your family in the future. Maybe it's time to gather all your "vital statistics" into one easily accessible package that you and others can find and use whenever they're needed.

Once you get the housekeeping items out of the way and recorded on your computer or written down in a logical, legible way, you can begin planning.

What do you expect to be doing a year from now? What would you *like* to be doing a year from now? Would you like to own a bed and breakfast in the south of France? If that's your goal and you believe it's attainable, write it down, and add the subheads that go with it. Write letters. Get brochures. Check competition. Research bed and breakfasts in the south of France. Take French lessons. Find out if the kids can go to school in the south of France. Check the French consulate for miscellaneous details. Get on the Net and talk to someone who's already in the business. What do people expect for breakfast in a bed and breakfast?

If there are other goals on the plate of possibles, note them. Is your career matching your talents these days? Maybe it's time for a *time* investment in the things you like to do, to hone your skills. If you believe you could make a go of it in photography, for instance, maybe it's time to get into night school for instruction that will take you from being merely good to being consistently excellent. Write it down, check it out.

You don't mind the company you're working for but you would rather be in the office in Duluth. Can it happen? Write it down and check it out.

How you organize things is up to you, but maybe you can slot your goals into categories that cover off such things as job, financial, kids, wife/husband. Be as specific as you can. If you want to keep it a secret, that's up to you, but others may be interested in knowing where you're hoping to go. Maybe you need the help of your husband/wife to make it all happen.

My only point in all this is to ask that you attempt to develop a clear sense of direction, to write it down, to be specific. It's another secret of success.

CHAPTER 13

The $60,000 Education

SECRET NO. 6: *Never consider the possibility of failure.* One more time? *Never consider the possibility of failure.* There are so many people who never make it in life because they go into something convinced they don't stand a chance. You know people like this and chances are their timidity drives you crazy. You want to say to them: "For goodness sake, you have *every* chance in the world. Go out there and *do it!*"

Start climbing mountains, running races, doing *anything* in the belief that you will fail and you will surely fail. It's guaranteed. Winners tell us they can *taste* victory. And they can. Winning sprinters visualize that moment when they will soar through the tape at the head of the pack. That's the way *I* saw it when I won the 880 as a kid in England. I didn't visualize failure. I saw and achieved glorious, triumphant victory.

P E T E R   L E G G E

You must have seen the reactions of all kinds of athletes in that moment of triumph. The victory dance in the end zone when the winning touchdown is made, the stomp of delight in tennis, the whoop of joy when the long putt goes in, the hugs in a soccer match. Yes! I, we will win, they all said and drove themselves to victory.

Failure? Get a life!

OK, you say, so what if I do all this and I come in second? What if someone else has the same approach to life. We can't *all* win. Sometimes we lose and sometimes we make mistakes. What then? We learn from our mistakes and we come back to race again.

Soon after our company was first established, one of my senior people made a mistake that cost us $60,000 on the bottom line. We were a small, growing company and $60,000 in those days was a lot of money. Heck, it's *still* a lot of money! We had a pretty serious talk about what had happened, how something like that could have been avoided, how vital it is to consider every angle when decisions of such consequence are being made.

Obviously upset, he handed me an envelope. I opened it and found his resignation. It took me a split second to respond.

"Resignation?" I said. "You've gotta be kidding. I've just invested $60,000 in your *education*! Get out of here and next time do it better."

Failure is an event – not a person. These are learning opportunities to know what to avoid in the future. I have heard it said that to double your success in life, you need to quadruple your failures and treat them as learning experiences.

We don't plan for or expect failure. We go in to win and we visualize victory. If we gird our loins to take the prize and we fail, so be it. There will be another day and the prize, *many* prizes, will be ours to savour.

Excellence can be attained if you...

1. ***Care more than others think is wise***
2. ***Risk more than others think is safe***
3. ***Expect more than others think is possible***
4. ***Dream more than others think is practical***

—Anonymous

CHAPTER 14

Education is Big Business

I'M ALWAYS TICKLED TO READ about seniors who return to university to get a first or second degree. At ages of 80 or 90, with mile-wide grins on their faces, these amazing people parade down the aisle with graduates who are invariably much younger than they are, to be "capped" in a ceremony that celebrates the attainment of new knowledge.

These are among the most heartwarming stories we can read because they have all the elements that we respond to so readily: courage, determination, the will to win, the realization that there's no limit to the capacity of our brains, that at any age, we human beings are always amazing creatures.

I think another reason we're so blown away by these stories is that many of us would like to think we could do the same. The trouble is, we're just too darned comfortable right at this moment. We can do it, we say, but next year or the year after will be a much more convenient time than right now. We'll get around to it. Absolutely. We'll get around to it.

My seventh secret for success is: *We must dedicate ourselves to continuing education.* No matter what form it may take, reading a book, returning to school, attending a seminar, night school, whatever, we all owe it to ourselves to add more knowledge to our lives. It's almost criminal to do otherwise.

You can dream about extending yourself in your present career or branching off into a new one, but unless you prepare yourself for change, it just won't happen; those mythical "breaks" will never come.

Seniors return to school because they know, or may have discovered late in life, that we're given these computers we call brains to load with exciting data that we call knowledge. And it can be an absolutely thrilling experience to start the process of bringing brains and data together.

Have you ever talked to someone who has gone back to complete a high school education? Not only do they delight in sharing their knowledge, but they have fire in their eyes and a longing for more of the same. They've primed the pump and they're ready to go!

Benjamin Franklin, who preferred turkeys over eagles and bravely captured the static of storms with nought but a kite, is supposed to have said: "If a man empties his purse into his head, no one can take it away from him. An investment in knowledge always pays the best interest." I couldn't verify the quote, but having read other snippets of his wisdom, it *does* sound like printer Ben.

My career and lifestyle means that time is mostly tight, but I try to read a book a week. That's about 50 a year, a small library of books in whatever lifetime is allotted to me. I can't possibly lose by doing what I'm doing and I know there are new thoughts and ideas being published all the time. If you haven't been into a bookstore lately or browsed the shelves of your local library you won't know that there are books about absolutely *everything*.

Borrow a book, if you must, but ideally *buy* it, because in your hands you will hold something of *value*. When you read it, keep a yellow marker in your hand and put a stripe of colour over the parts you believe are important, that are actionable, that you can easily find again. Make the books you read *tools* that can help you to build a better you.

You don't have time? Make a little time. I remember discussing this issue in one of the *Insights* that I present to my staff each week. You can steal some time from your sleep and never even notice it, I said. Set your alarm 15 minutes earlier every week for a month. At the end of the month, you'll be getting up an hour earlier and gaining nine extra weeks of time every year! Nine weeks of reading or any other kind of learning? Pure luxury.

I could go on with time-saving opportunities, but that's not my point right now. What I'm suggesting you do is make a commitment of any kind to your continuing education.

If at first you don't succeed, you're about average, because like commitment to an exercise program or anything else that's tough to do, it ain't easy. There's no promise of instant results or, for that matter, of *any* results. But there's a very good chance that one day you'll wake up to discover that formal learning has given you the kind of self-confidence you once thought belonged only to others, that you're more comfortable with new and interesting conversation, that you have opinions that get other people thinking, that you command new respect. And all of this, not surprisingly, gives you the confidence to stretch yourself even further.

Education, as you may have already observed, is huge business. Not only because, as a society, we know it's important, but because the "market" demands it. So often I've heard people say that if they had the money they would go back to school, if they won the lottery, they would get an education. Education of any kind constantly beckons and all those books, all that knowledge are there for the taking. You don't have to win lotteries to get started. It's as simple as saying: "OK, Pete, I'll get myself a book and a yellow marker and I'll do it today."

No one but *you* can begin to *reshape* you and it does happen one step at a time. Start uploading some new knowledge today. It will remain with you always as gigabytes of pure, personal gold.

CHAPTER 15

In Praise of Workaholics

YOU MAY OCCASIONALLY GET FLAK from your family about those late nights at the office, but you won't get it from me. No. 8 on my list of Secrets for Success is: *Develop a workaholic mentality.* Sorry, but it has to be. It takes time to create the world you want, and it's time you must invest in your goals, your future.

A 40-hour work week is very rare among high achievers. Sixty, even 80, is more common. I devote substantially more than 40 hours a week to my business and my career – and I still find time for my family, for recreation, for interests that are not work related. (I'd be dead without a round of golf now and then!) My work is not an interruption to my day.

I suppose the key to deciding how much time we should spend at work depends a lot on how well we *manage* our time, and how *fast* we can do things while we're in our work environment. Thankfully, some of the very big decisions can be made in minutes, and time is used very effectively and efficiently.

Other decisions take much longer because we question the direction we're going and these questions generate more questions, more research, and the need for more decisions. And it all takes more time.

If you've developed a new product and you believe the time and markets are ripe, dozens, perhaps hundreds, of people must get involved. As you get closer to your launch, you can expect to burn the midnight oil night after night. As a team leader, being there, being "hands on" is a necessary part of the process. You have to see it through and the hours mount.

The term workaholic, like alcoholic, is interpreted negatively. But the accuracy of the word is questionable. Being a workaholic suggests that, no matter what, we are driven by work for work's sake. Sometimes that *is* the case. I've known lots of people who work long hours, but they do it to escape from something else.

"I have to get back to the office," they tell their spouses and families. "Don't quite know when I'll be home."

And when they get there, all they do is shuffle paper. They have absolutely no reason to be there. Regretfully, it's an escape. People like this sometimes do nothing for years and years. They need to get back on track, perhaps through career counselling, job evaluation or a long chat with a counsellor, mentor or close friend. As I've said many times, you can't fool yourself and no amount of time at the office or other "work" can change this.

The kind of workaholic mentality I'm talking about is the one in which you have your plan in place and you work for as long as it takes to make the plan succeed.

A workaholic mentality means sticking with the program until it's done, start to finish. No goofing off. No ragged edges. Wrap it up neat and tidy.

A workaholic mentality means digging deeper to make things work, being creative in reaching your goal, being clever enough to look in from the outside to ask yourself: "Is there another, *better* way?"

The rewards of a workaholic mentality are whatever you want them to be. When the job is done, take the vacation you promised yourself. Go big, do something you and everyone else in your circle will remember for a long time. Move into your first home, your second or your really big third. Do it because it was in your plan and the reward was part of the goal.

I work often with companies that set corporate goals for sales and promise big rewards for everyone involved. There's no messing around, no broken promises. Everyone knows the rules and everyone knows that the rewards after weeks or months of hard teamwork will be great. It's human nature to be attracted by a carrot on a stick. We're all expected to give of ourselves, no matter what, but it's amazing how much better things are when there's an incentive of some kind at the end of the road.

Winners who end up with paid trips to exotic places that were incentives for sales goals have enormous appreciation for the company that made it happen. They come back refreshed and ready for more of the same.

If you're *thinking* like a president to achieve success, you'll *work* like a president. And take it from me, presidents work hard indeed.

CHAPTER 16

The Winner's Circle

SUCCESS SECRET NO. 9: *Stay close to the winners, stay clear of the losers.* It may be cruel, but you can waste a lot of time and be drained of a ton of energy if you persist in mingling with the wrong people or the wrong crowd.

It takes about a minute to pick up on the attitude of a loser. These are the people who have never made it, have never even *begun* to make it. But they will give you a hundred reasons why the world is impeding their progress to fame and fortune. They blame society, the government, the boss, their families, their very genes. They whine, they suck you dry of energy and ideas and still they remain unchanged.

I think these kinds of people do more harm to our society and our business world than just about anyone else. The naysayers, the turkeys, the negative thinkers – stay clear of them, whatever you do, because they'll rob you blind of your enthusiasm, your sense of purpose, your ideals and principles. Let them wallow in their own pessimistic view of life.

I'm not suggesting that you become a groupie in the circle of the rich, famous and fabulous . . . not exactly. If you spot an admirable trait in a workmate, cling a little closer, share the enthusiasm, add to the good idea, be supported by people who appreciate the things you're doing. Steer yourself toward the A Team and the winners' circle. Winning is infectious.

Don't be afraid to be a copycat. We all do it and benefit from it. If there's something you see that's admirable, work on something to match it in your own program. Reject the losers, copy the winners. If you observe a better way that a winner gets from A to B, take the same route or better.

Contribute, if you're able, to the winner's continuing success. You won't lose by doing it, and the rewards will come back in spades.

CHAPTER 17

Be Teachable

SECRET NO. 10? Quite simply: *Be teachable*. You don't know everything and you never will. But you owe it to yourself and to your success to absorb knowledge and ideas now and for as long as you live. There's no end to your ability to learn from others and from the world around you.

You've heard people say: "I know everything I need to know." What on earth are they talking about? You've heard them say: "Why do I need travel? It's all on television." Excuse me?

Every day of our lives we have the opportunity to learn something new, to expose ourselves to written or spoken words or images that can benefit our lives and contribute to our potential success.

Be teachable in an informal way, be teachable in a formal way. If you're content to read and look at pictures that are all pap, you're doing yourself a tremendous injustice. If you believe your tool for education is nothing more than a device to surf channels, you're missing out on enormous opportunity and you don't *deserve* to succeed.

There are so many benefits to being a teachable person. As noted in the previous chapter, doesn't it make sense to listen more carefully to the winners, to be open and to learn from those who have obviously succeeded?

Vancouver businessman Jimmy Pattison, whom I've written about before, has accumulated enormous wealth, achieved phenomenal success, and contributed much to his community. He once told me that those who have the capacity to dream big dreams also have the capacity to *accomplish* those dreams.

Isn't that great news? What a wealth of wisdom lies in that one sentence. If ever I'm in doubt, I just take Jimmy's advice and dream a bigger dream. I wouldn't believe for a minute that Jimmy would ever shut himself out to new knowledge. He's teachable and flexible and, I might add, one tough cookie.

I've said before that everything counts. I've talked about Socrates' law of cause and effect, that you have it within you to change things. If you're not happy with the effect, you can change the cause. You can be born in poverty, but you don't have to stay there. You can be fired from your job, but there will be another opportunity tomorrow or the next day, or the day after that. Maybe it means you'll need some retraining. Maybe it means that this time around you will take the route you were meant to take the first time around.

Be teachable. Be ready for change at any time. Welcome it and run with it. Look at the world with wider eyes, see yourself as others see you, be ready to admit with honesty that someone else may have a better idea.

I spend a lot of time listening to the philosophy of others on audio tapes. If you're a commuter, or use your car for work, you might like to try it. I figure that in any given year, many of us spend as much as three months in our cars. Automobiles must have a greater purpose than merely getting us from A to B.

Look at your car as a university on wheels and grab yourself some tapes that will educate and motivate you. You'll arrive at your destination refreshed, almost unaware that you had to fight your way through traffic. You'll have new insights, new strength, a new sense of purpose.

Be teachable. On the road of asphalt and on the road of life.

Practice so much they think
you are lucky.

—Anonymous

CHAPTER 18

Peak of Perfection

SUCCESS SECRET NO. 11: *Be prepared to climb from peak to peak.* If you've ever been to the top of a mountain, you know how exhilarating it can be. Mountains and other high places lift us above the plain and let us survey our world from a new and vaulted position. It's different up there. All the mediocrity seems to drop away, and in the clean air we can breathe deeply a world that's fresher and more spiritually rewarding, where we rise above the routine and feel our hearts swell with the strength of achievement.

Mountaintop experiences, unfortunately, are not served up with any regularity. You have to have the gear and the intent to start climbing.

Some people believe their mountaintop experiences will be given to them. They buy a lottery ticket, then sit back and wait for the big moment. And despite the fact that "you never know," the moment rarely comes. And time slips by and life goes on.

Moses had some very real mountaintop experiences because he was ready to go after them and receive them when he found them. He had his moment with God on a mountain which must have been the highest of highs! But despite this one big event, Moses spent a lot of time slogging through the trenches. He too found that life is complex and often difficult.

We go to the mountaintops and climb from peak to peak because we can challenge ourselves to do exactly that and because "they're there." We do it because we know that the view from the top will be spectacular, a place where we can not only rest and relish the achievement of the climb, but we can focus on the next beckoning range that lies beyond and identify our next potential conquest.

Once you begin, once you discover the heady rewards the peaks can bring, I guarantee you'll be a mountain climber for the rest of your life.

CHAPTER 19

Roll With the Punches

SUCCESS SECRET NO. 12: *Develop resilience.* It's amazing how often we humans get beat up on our journey through life. When we least expect it, wham! pow! biff! Most of the time the scars aren't too obvious, but it can sure hurt inside. Thin, brave smiles hide all kinds of grief.

What we must learn to do when adversity hits with a left hook, right jab or a well-aimed uppercut is to bounce back from the punches.

"That hurt, but I'm not going to let it happen again!"

Adversity has a way of teaching us some good lessons. Hit your finger with a hammer and for the rest of your life you're more careful with a hammer.

Experience a heart attack, and, unless you're very silly indeed, you will change your life. That means changing the way you deal with people, changing your diet, beginning an exercise program. All these things contribute to a stronger heart, to more resilience, to a person more able to come back stronger when adversity takes a whack at you, when opportunity knocks.

And nothing will ever be the same again. Cancer taught me that. *I* will certainly never be the same again.

We can go either way when we've been physically or emotionally damaged. We can lie down and sulk for the rest of our lives or we can pick ourselves up, dust ourselves off and start all over again.

Let me assure you that when you *do* start again, you will begin with a whole lot of energy you never thought you had, with rules that you wrote yourself, with goals that are more clear, with focus that you have pulled more tightly.

It's quite wonderful. Yesterday's bad news is quickly forgotten, because the road ahead has wide open lanes that are full of promise.

CHAPTER 20

Creative Problem Solving

IF YOU WERE TO SIT DOWN right now and list the three biggest problems that are driving you crazy, I bet within 24 hours you will have figured a way to solve two of them – and maybe all three.

Why? Because if you think your problems through, cover off all the potential variables that will help you find a solution, seek the advice of others, maybe share the experience so you're not alone tackling what may seem like the impossible, you'll figure out a way to do it. You will creatively make it happen.

We've all had crises in our lives. We've all had to suddenly take on something we thought impossible and we've had to solve it. There was no one else to do it; the decision rested with us alone. And you know what? We worked it out. Do this, this and this and there you are. It's done.

Secret No. 13: *Unlock your inborn creativity.*

Many of us work for, or have worked for, government agencies or other large corporations or organizations. If we were down on the lowest rungs of the corporate ladder, chances are we tended to let others make the decisions because we felt we didn't count, or original thought was not encouraged.

But now you're the president of a company that is *you*. Now it's *your* deal because it's *your* life and *your* success we're talking about. Now you're self-employed and, most of the time, there's no one else to make the decisions.

Margaret Thatcher, despite her sometimes prickly manner, was a great prime minister. She once said that leaders are where they should be. They're lonely because they're out front leading. Margaret Thatcher found out that at the top there is no one else.

Being out front, having all that responsibility, means you can now be tested. Unless you ask for input from others, the decision now rests with you. You want to paint the plant green? Paint it green. You want to deal with this bank and not that bank? Deal away. You want to add a shift, play a round of golf, fly to New York to the trade show? Your decision.

While you will learn to savour the experience of life at the top of your personal corporation, you will, if you want to make it through, share the decision-making process with others. But that's a whole other story.

The point of *this* secret is that you can solve problems, clear away the guff, get on with the things that are important, maximize your energy and turn it in the best directions.

Take a break from this book and go to it. Right now!

CHAPTER 21

Be An Unshakable Optimist

SECRET NO. 14, AND IT COULD BE my favourite, is *be an unshakable optimist.* I hope that's what I am.

I always believe that the sun will shine for the picnic, that I'll meet the impossible deadline, that I'll surpass my personal and corporate goals, that my favourite team will win the championship. Why think any other way? I don't ever plan for failure. If, by chance, something goes wrong, I tackle that opportunity when it happens.

Athletes psyche themselves for victory, not for defeat. If you say: "But what if I lose?" the thought will return again and again. Visualize the tape at the end of the track and run for it!

My wife, my beautiful, bubbly, vivacious, sexy wife came into my life as a much different person than she is today. The woman I married was not raised in an environment that instilled self-confidence and self-worth. How many people have you met who have suffered the same fate in *their* upbringing?

But Kay wasn't content to stay in that condition for the rest of her life. She would change, as she had every right to.

Four years ago, when our kids had matured and could look after themselves, she said: "Honey, I have to do something meaningful. I have to take on a big dream."

"Like . . .?"

"I've got to go back to university and get a degree."

She was certain in an uncertain kind of way.

"You know that's going to take three-and-a-half years," she said. "I'll be three-and-a-half years older when I finish."

"Sweetheart," said I, "you're going to be three-and-a-half years older, no matter *what* you do."

She graduated last December with a B.A. in Religious Education.

Being unshakably optimistic is about determination and positive self-talk. It's saying you can do it. Kay's return to university was a struggle for both of us, but she did it, we did it and you can do it.

Have you ever talked to yourself in the mirror? Have you ever stood naked in front of a mirror and said to that face and body: "You, despite your large tummy, your wrinkles and your greying hair, are unstoppable. Get yourself dressed and take on the world!"

Talk to yourself, give endless praise to your brilliance, your ability to do absolutely anything.

Kay tells me that we preach and teach the things we most need to hear ourselves. That certainly applies to me. I'm up, because I make more than a hundred presentations a year that reflect an optimistic message. How can I be anything else but up unless I'm deceiving myself? And why do that?

I have to hear what I'm talking about. I have to hear myself. I have to continually remind myself to recharge my batteries, to get motivated, get stimulated.

Self-talk. It is *so* important. Let me remind you again that of the five or so billion people who occupy this planet, there is no one exactly like you.

And Kay… well she is now on to an even bigger dream, her Master's degree in Theology and Counselling. I couldn't be more proud of her accomplishments.

You can accomplish miracles. And eternal optimism will help you to make them happen.

*The secret of success
is constancy to purpose.*
—Benjamin Disraeli
19th-century Prime Minister of Great Britain

CHAPTER 22

A Wise Word From the Greeks

MY DICTIONARY SAYS THAT Mentor was a friend of Odysseus and tutor to his son Telemachus. While this piece of history is all Greek to me, I respect it because from Mentor, we got the word mentor, without the capital M. And a mentor, like the original, is a trusted friend and adviser.

Which leads me to Secret No. 15: *Find a mentor or mentors.* We've already learned that it can be lonely at the top. But your life will be substantially improved if you share your thoughts, dreams and goals with someone else. Like a mentor.

A mentor is a person who is willing to listen to you babble about your plans, good and not so good. This is the person, often removed from your immediate circle, who can sit with you on a river bank and offer words of wisdom and a good ear. You buy him or her lunch and you say: "I think I know where I'm going, but I need your help to find the way." And they will help you.

I've met lots of mentors in my travels. Mostly they stay in the background, doing nothing but absorbing the scene. But they're there, as solid as the Rock of Gibraltar, never wavering in their loyalty, supportive to the end.

Get yourself a mentor, a person who is often a bit older and certainly a lot wiser than you are, who believes in you and wants you to succeed. He or she will ask much of you and vice versa, but the relationship will never be parent-child; it will be adult-adult and friend-friend. A good mentor can lift a ton of stress from your shoulders in a split second.

"Tell me about your plans."

"I think everything's going to work out exactly as you think it will."

"Do you really believe that's the way you should go?"

Mentors will always give you the straight goods, bring you back into line, make sure you're being honest with yourself and those around you.

You will leave every meeting with your mentor feeling that there has been progress, that you have shared something important and your direction remains clear. They will never share your secrets.

Those Greeks have a lot of good things going!

CHAPTER 23

Just Do It

SECRET NO. 16: *DO IT NOW!* Don't put it off, because tomorrow will be too late. Write that letter *now.* Say I'm sorry *now.* Say I love you *now.* Offer that word of encouragement *now.* Read that book *now.* Procrastination is not only the thief of time, but so often the contributor to failure.

Why wait? Step up to the front and say: "Pick *me!*" Grab a moment and fill it with something useful, even if it's only to sniff a rose or taste a new brew of coffee. But do it *now.*

"I'll do it next week. Promise!" You know you won't.

The time to do anything is right now and the satisfaction in doing exactly that is tremendous. Wrap it up, put it to bed, finish it, go the extra mile and make it great.

There are all kinds of opportunities to "do it now" in your business day. Try a few of them.

When the mail hits your desk or your home in the morning, try acting on all of it. You *know* the bill has to be paid. Pay it. Why are you putting that magazine offer on the think-about-it-later pile. You know *right now* whether you want it or not. If you don't act *right now* you'll be shuffling that piece of paper around for the next six weeks – at which stage you'll chuck it anyway.

If you're planning to succeed, you'll need some precision in your life. That means more hustle, less time spent on the little things, much more on the things that count.

Do it now. Clear your metaphoric desk to make way for the good, big stuff that's coming your way.

CHAPTER 24

Honestly, One Step at a Time

BE IMPECCABLY HONEST WITH *yourself and with others.* That's
Secret No. 17. If you're anything *but* that, you may as well quit
right now and join the low lifers.

Be honest with your family, your spouse, your kids, your
company, your community, your country. Respect the values you
believe in. Honesty in all your dealings should never be a question that needs to slow you down. At the end of the road, or anywhere along the way, you'll be able to hold your head high and
say you did it in your own, *honest* way.

I know you have a lot on your plate, but Secret No. 18 says
that success comes when you *concentrate singlemindedly on just
one thing at a time.*

We are victims these days of a ton of messages of all kinds.

They come in the mail, in memos, in faxes, in phone calls and e-mail from around the world. The paperwork piles up on our desks or wherever our work station may be. The sales report *has* to be read, production *demands* an ASAP answer, you *have to* get the oil changed in your car. And so on.

Of course all these things must happen, but what you *have to do* is arrange the *have to's* into a list of manageable priorities.

Tackle the projects one at a time and move on. You just can't do them all at once and come up with effective solutions. Focus on one thing at a time, work it through, move on to the next thing. Determine quickly what is important. And for goodness sake, don't forget the milk on the way home!

CHAPTER 25

Life at the Fat Farm

SECRET NO. 19: *GET SERIOUS.* Seriously. Get serious about being decisive, about taking responsibility for your life, about your determination to succeed, about your business, about your need for knowledge, about your kids, your marriage, your health.

I have a number of Achilles heels, but my persistent downfall is that I tend to gain weight at the drop of a mashed potato. I said earlier in this book that everything counts and what I put in my mouth *really* counts. I get heavier. I go on a diet for two weeks and lose not a gram. (See *being honest with one's self!*)

Before Christmas, I said to my wife Kay: "Sweetheart, I *have* to lose weight." Not surprisingly, she agreed. Who wants to cuddle with a live Pillsbury doughboy?

So we treated ourselves to a Palm Springs fat farm. My goal was to lose 15 pounds before the upcoming British Columbia

Variety Club Telethon in which I was to participate as an on-camera principal. Cameras don't flatter you. In my case, they have a default button that makes me both shorter and wider!

I lost 18 pounds at the fat farm. Starvation at an enormous price! But a goal achieved, even if I have to fight fat for the rest of my life!

Everything counts. You, me, all of us can not allow ourselves to ever look back and say: "If only . . ." We have a responsibility to stop the "if only" thing before it ever gets a chance to start.

Attack your challenges and opportunities with gusto. Get serious about all the things that count. Revel in your achievements, take on bigger challenges and savour the victories.

Secret No. 20 logically follows: *self-discipline.* This is where character is built. Do the things you have to do, even when you don't want to do them. I hate working out, but I have to do it. I'd much rather play a round of golf, drink a couple of beers, do *anything* but spend 20 minutes working out. Yuk!

Self-discipline is the foundation of our character.

You, I'm sure, have your own secret horrors. I sympathize with you. But practise self-discipline. Work out. Don't make a mess in the bathroom.

(Isn't golf exercise? Why do I have to work out when I play golf? Hmm?)

CHAPTER 26

Dinner with Chuck and Di

WHEN YOU DO SOMETHING for someone else, the same or more will be done for you. That's one way of describing Secret No. 21, which I call the *universal law of reciprocity.*

What is it? It's give and take, an equation that balances itself.

For instance? If you speak negatively about someone, some organization, some company on one side of the equation, the same thing will come back at you from the other side. Not necessarily from the same people *you've* been talking about, but by *someone.* Sow and ye shall reap.

Conversely, when you do something nice for someone else, something nice will be done for you. Most of the time, the process happens without our knowledge, but believe me, it happens. It has happened to me so often that I've lost track.

Every year, I work 22 straight hours on the Variety Club

Telethon, scream around the world making speeches, and meet hundreds of people – not because I want anything back, but because I *love doing it*. Heck, if I didn't have to eat, I would do it for nothing! (Those who know me may say, so stop eating! I'll disregard the insult.)

My point is, all these things I love doing bring me reciprocal benefits. Maybe not right then, but *some time*, often when I least expect it. It's the law of reciprocity.

Knowing this law exists, I tend to say "thank you" a lot. I write a lot of thank-you letters; I express my appreciation when people go out of their way to help me; I don't speak unkindly of others, be they individuals or companies.

A story to illustrate all this? I once tried to make a sale to a man named David Bentall, part of a family that has built most of downtown Vancouver. "Most" is an exaggeration, but the Bentall family has done a lot of wonderful things.

Anyway, David wasn't buying, but part way through the pitch, he said: "You know, I want to do something for my father. He's 80, he's been recognized with the Order of Canada, among other honours, but my efforts to do more have been denied by the board members. They say we can't spend any more money on public demonstration."

I was aware of the substantial philanthropic contributions Clarke Bentall had made to the Vancouver community and, as a member of the board of the Variety Club, I submitted his name as a candidate for the Variety Club Community Golden Heart Achievement Award, the highest award the Variety Club bestows.

I was delighted when the nomination was accepted.

Not surprisingly (put your effort where your mouth is, Legge!), I was asked to chair the event that would honour him. For a year, I met every Wednesday with David Bentall to plan the dinner, to sell the tickets and arrange the entertainment. We lined up Bob Hope as principal entertainer and organized a number of supporting speakers. In due course, the event took place.

It was a wonderful evening and, through our combined efforts, we raised $160,000 for Variety's special kids. And, in the course of the planning, I had found a new friend in David Bentall. I was completely satisfied with the whole affair and wanted nothing more.

Three months later, David asked if I could meet him for breakfast. Absolutely, I said, suddenly remembering that I still hadn't been able to sell him an ad in any of our magazines.

We met as good friends and, halfway through the meal, he said: "I just want to thank you sincerely for what you did for my father."

"The pleasure was ours," I said. "We did it for your dad, but we also did it for Variety's special needs kids."

"There's something else . . ."

I brightened, and, while I hadn't asked for it, I sensed that a sale was imminent.

"Somewhere during our year together, you said you were fascinated and charmed by Prince Charles and Diana, the Princess of Wales."

"I am," I said. "Lovely couple."

"How would you like to have dinner with them?"

"I . . ."

He extended his hand. "Here are airline tickets for you and your wife to Toronto. You'll be having dinner with Prince Charles and Diana, the Princess of Wales."

I gulped. "Can I call him Chuck?"

I was absolutely thrilled. The law of reciprocity had worked again on the grandest of scales.

It's a true and wonderful story. And who knows, one day David may yet buy an ad!

Previous page:
It was a race I thought would be impossible to win — the killer half mile at Tavistock Hall. But at the age of 12, I discovered a reserve of inner strength, and pushed on to miraculous victory. In my cricket "whites," trophy in hand, and my proud mother beside me, it was one of the great "photo ops" and moments of my life.

This page:
Never did a couple look more charming than this one. My parents on their wedding day at Greenford in Middlesex. I was just three, below left, when I got my first car, obviously built for kids with very long legs. Two years later I was riding Buttons, my first horse. And come to think of it, my last.

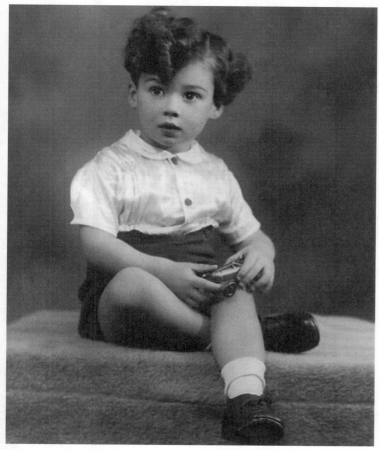

The Big Race at Tavistock Hall attracted a substantial gallery, all of whom helped to spur me on to victory in the half mile. That's my grandmother on the far left, my mother, father, me on Dad's lap, and members of my mother's family. At left, and sporting several pounds of very curly hair, this was my first "formal" at the age of three.

I have talked a lot in this book about Tavistock Hall Preparatory School for Boys. It is one of those uniquely British institutions that somehow had what was needed to guide kids like me into adulthood, to teach me about values, principles, rules for life. This painting, by Juliet Murray, is used with permission. Kay and I, left, were married in London on Nov. 23, 1969. I seem to have been much shorter then.

Our family has been involved for years with Young Life and the organization's spectacular Camp Malibu, on an inlet north of Vancouver. Malibu is a place that enriches the soul, washes away the stresses of the city. You can see Malibu's benefits in the faces of Kay and me, left, the fun of it all, below, with our daughters Samantha, Rebecca and Amanda. A few years later, we snapped our girls in Hawaii.

Throughout several careers, I've brushed often with show-biz types. At left, Vancouver talk show host Dave Abbott and I were all smiles with that tragi-comic lady Jayne Mansfield. On the set of an ABC-TV pilot in London, below left, sporting monumental sideburns and a substantial set of glasses, I pondered my future with Engelbert Humperdinck. A new pair of glasses and several years later, I met Milton Berle at a Variety Clubs International convention in Los Angeles. Below left, I graduated from Disney University, got to meet Mickey and wear his ears. Below right, wearing even longer sideburns and the noisiest jacket, I was MC at a roast for British Columbia Premier Dave Barrett.

British Prime Minister Margaret Thatcher, whom I much admire, and husband Dennis were guests at the opening of the UK Pavilion at Expo 86 in Vancouver (left). At the same prime ministerial level, that's me with Canadian Prime Minister Jean Chretien (below). In for a fund-raiser, Her Royal Highness Princess Elizabeth of Yugoslavia joined me for a picture (top right). Countess Mountbatten of Burma (right bottom) helps celebrate the Canadian Red Cross 100th birthday on her visit to Vancouver. I'm wearing the uniform of the Order of St. John of Jerusalem.

Over the years, my work with Variety Clubs International has been a labour of love and every February I look forward to being part of the Variety Club Telethon, produced by BCTV and which, since 1966, has raised more than $57 million for Variety's special kids. Friends I've met along the way have included, left, Ray Charles, right, Monty Hall and below, Second World War songstress Dame Vera Lynn.

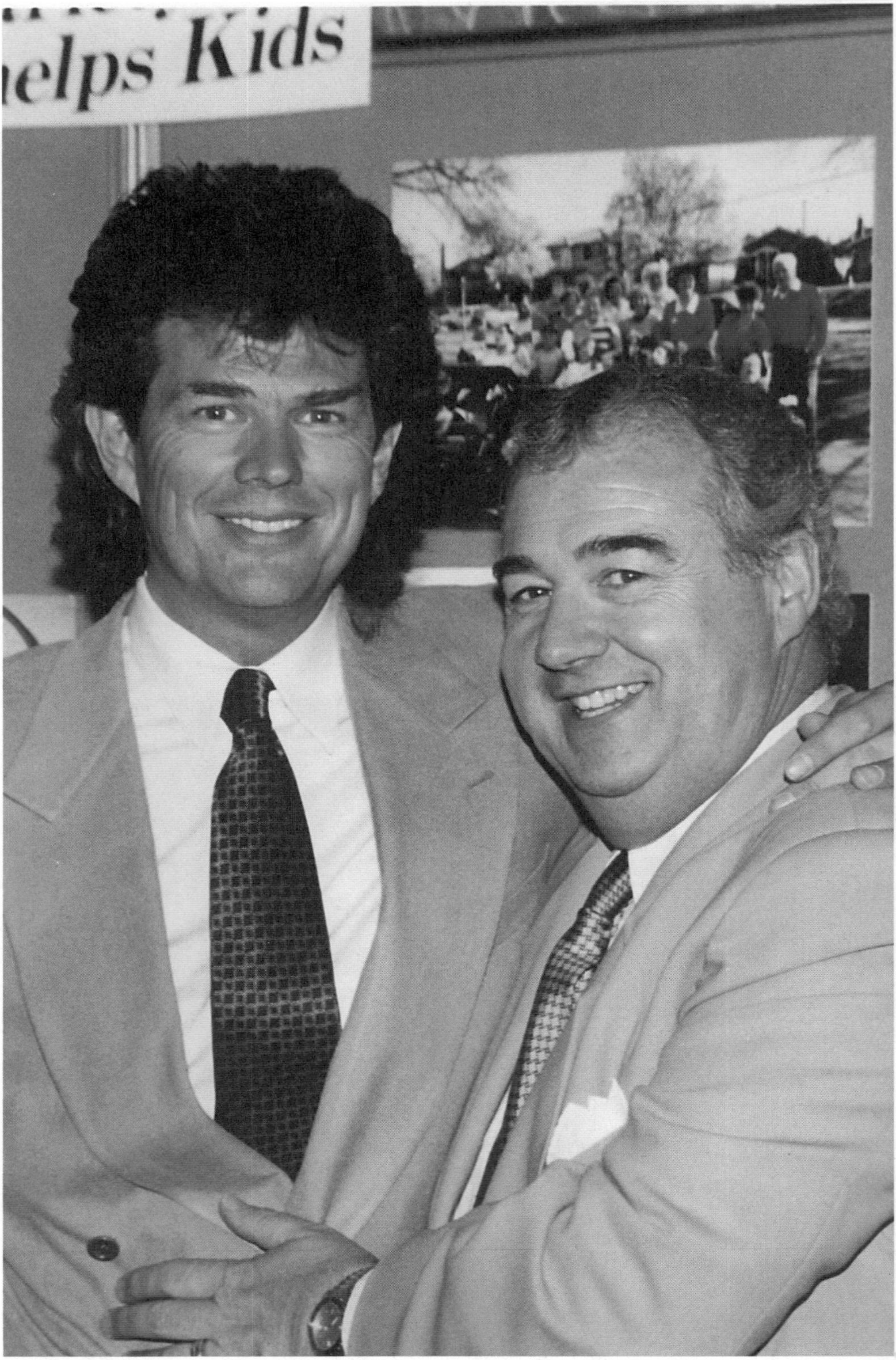
elps Kids

The guy behind any number of sensational singing successes is, left, Grammy Award-winning composer, arranger, producer David Foster. I discovered golf late in my life and enjoy every moment I can spend with a club in my hand. People like PGA Seniors champ Ray Floyd are an inspiration. So, too, is the legendary Bob Hope, below, with me and my Canada Wide Magazines & Communications partner, Neil Soper.

More Variety Club Telethon activity, at far left I'm with Bionic Woman Lindsay Wagner, Police Woman Angie Dickinson, left, and Gilligan's Island woman Dawn Wells, below, whom you may remember better as Mary Ann. *Following page:* Tall enough to be a candidate for the NBA is His Royal Highness King Kagan V of Rwanda, who came to Vancouver to help us raise $185,000 for the Canadian Red Cross and the victims of the Rwandan civil war.

CHAPTER 27

Is the Mike On?

I ONCE READ THAT THE NO. 1 fear of many businessmen and women is not the fear of death, but the fear of standing in front of an audience to make a speech. Their palms sweat and the hair bristles at the back of their necks at the very thought of it.

I respect their fear. But as someone who earns a living making speeches year-round in front of audiences large and small and loves every minute of it, I don't *understand* their fear.

For me, speechmaking is like a shot of adrenalin. Before I ever open my mouth or my mike in front of a crowd, I can feel the energy coming back. A huge wave of friendly feeling surges from people who seem quite ready to receive me and whatever my message may be. Really.

If I'm in an audience and the chair says: "Ladies and gentlemen, will you please give a big hometown welcome to today's keynote speaker . . ." I'm ready to open my arms to whatever's coming. Why not?

Which leads me to Secret No. 22. *Learn to be an accomplished speaker.* I'm not suggesting that you need to pursue it at quite the pace I do, but speaking well, being able to express yourself in any kind of forum, will do wonders for your self-esteem and contribute enormously to your chances for success.

Those same people who are afraid of speaking in front of an audience may not even realize that they already make all kinds of "speeches" to all kinds of audiences: the audience of one who is a loans officer in a bank; the audience of one who is a doctor; the audience of one who is a waiter in a restaurant; the audience of three who may be their workmates.

Just before I started writing this chapter, I was giving words of encouragement to a woman who desperately wanted to be president of her local gardening association. But there was absolutely no way she would permit her name to be placed in nomination because winning would have meant making an acceptance speech – and all those speeches that would follow during her presidential tenure. How unfortunate.

A fear of speaking in public greater than a fear of dying? This means that, at a funeral, you'd rather be in the casket than giving the eulogy! Yikes!

It really shouldn't be that way. Check out your local Toastmasters club and listen to the success stories. Get on board and discover the secrets that will make speechmaking possible, even enjoyable.

Watch the pros who pop up from time to time on PBS and other networks. Watch their timing, the words they use, the gestures, study the visual aids. Stop by your local courthouse and listen to the defence lawyer plead the case for the town's worst scoundrel.

Once you've overcome your public-speaking fears, there will be no stopping you. Point me to the microphone, you will say, and I'll knock 'em dead!

I know that, for some, it just isn't that easy. But begin, as you begin with *all* of the secrets in this book, and you will surely succeed.

And I'll be there in the front row applauding the loudest.

Act enthusiastic and you'll become enthusiastic

—Dale Carnegie

CHAPTER 28

Give Something Back

SECRET NO. 23: *DEVOTE PART OF YOUR time to your community.* Give some of your spare time – many say 25 per cent – to a charity that means something to you, that touches your heart. By doing so, the charity will benefit and *you* will benefit.

How will you benefit? Once you've decided to volunteer to become chair of the Red Cross lunch or whatever, other things come into play. You'll have to write a business plan, put a budget together, organize a team to help you, sell tables and a lot of other demanding tasks.

After the first few rejections, you will sharpen your selling skills, learn more about interaction with others, learn more people skills. (Do all these things have applications in business? Of course they do.) And you won't want to fail because you've told the Red Cross that you will deliver 200-plus people to the luncheon and you'd better have them!

Along the way you will develop a bit of a celebrity status. You may not be seeking it, but it will happen anyway. In your community, it's not all bad being a hometown hero when the lunch goes over the top.

I've worked for all kinds of charitable fund-raisers – telethons, golf tournaments, gala dinners, one-time events, fund drives – and there's no doubt at all that I've received much more by this involvement than I have ever given.

People have said: "Why would a 53-year-old man spend 22 hours doing a telethon?" And I say: "Because I believe in the cause and I love what I'm doing. It's also a great way to spend a weekend."

Give more of yourself and expect nothing in return. But get ready to be gracious when the returns start rolling in.

CHAPTER 29

Light on the Starch

SECRET NUMBER 24: JUST ONE WORD. *Commitment.* A commitment to give of your very best, no matter what, no matter where, no matter when.

Remember Joe Darion's great award-winning Broadway song from *Man of La Mancha* back in the 1960s?

The Quest — The Impossible Dream

To dream the impossible dream,

To fight the unbeatable foe,

To bear with unbearable sorrow,

To run where the brave dare not go.

To right the unrightable wrong,

To love pure and chaste from afar,

To try when your arms are too weary,

To reach the unreachable star.

This is my quest, to follow that star,

No matter how hopeless,

No matter how far;

To fight for the right without question or pause,

To be willing to march into hell for a heavenly cause . . .

Now *that's* some kind of commitment!

Sheila Murray Bethel is an internationally acclaimed professional speaker. In her best-selling book, *Making a Difference,* she describes commitment as perhaps inspired by a heavenly cause or by one of those rare moments that can change your life.

- If you've stood in line on graduation day, wearing cap and gown, to receive a certificate for a degree, you know what commitment is.

- If you've put a key into the front door of the biggest house or the tiniest condo that has just become yours, you know what commitment is.

- If you've stood in the Citizenship Court of your adopted country and taken a solemn oath, you know what commitment is.

- If your hand has been squeezed by the frail hand of a dying parent and you've heard the whispered words: "I love you more than life itself. I did the best I could," that's commitment.

- If your fellow workers finally reach a long-term goal.

- If you took the risk to start your own business – you understand commitment.

Life is short and life can be so sweet, but we *have* to make commitments to things we believe in, to values we must consistently pursue, to the quality things that we admire and respect.

It's a bit frivolous, but here's a little story.

I have difficulty finding shirts that fit. I have difficulty because I'm chubby, because I sweat a bit when I'm speaking in public – it's not nervousness, it's the physical gesticulations! – because travel can wear and tear shirts more than just about anything else can, because my heavy, fast-growing beard wears at the collars.

I like French cuffs. They're distinctive but their distinctiveness exposes them and they too wear out quickly. When shirts are laundered on the road, the cuffs take a real beating. And the buttons get bashed to bits in short order. I need shirts with collars, cuffs and buttons made of steel.

I once was on the road and ended up in a shirt shop. I said to the guy behind the counter: "I need shirts with collars, cuffs and buttons made of steel. Or something close."

"If I could find you a shirt like that, would you buy more than one?" he asked. I liked him already.

"Absolutely," I said.

He leaped to the top shelf and grabbed a shirt and opened it up on the table in front of me. He got a pad of steel wool – no kidding! – and started working on the collar. Backwards and forwards for what seemed like 15 minutes. The collar survived admirably.

He Brillo padded the cuffs with the same enthusiasm. Not a

mark. I started to pull out my wallet.

He got a hammer, a *hammer,* and started banging at the buttons. One, two, three, four, five, six, seven. Whack, whack, whack. They shone unscathed.

"I'll take a dozen," I said, and slapped down my credit card. The price was ridiculously high, but I was glad to pay for the commitment of the shirtmaker, to the commitment of the keener who made that most impressive sale.

The shirts have been marvellous, and have survived hundreds of washings with never a broken button. The collars and French cuffs sparkle ceaselessly in the spotlight.

I'm committed to quality. There's no other way.

CHAPTER 30

e

Never, Never, Never, Never Give Up

SECRET NUMBER 25: PERSEVERANCE. Former United States President Calvin Coolidge once said:

"Nothing in this world can take the place of persistence. Talent will not; nothing is more common than unsuccessful people with talent.

Genius will not; unrewarded genius is almost a proverb.

Education will not; the world is full of educated derelicts.

Persistence and determination alone are omnipotent.

The slogan "press on" has solved, and always will solve, the problems of the human race.

What we need in business, family, faith and the community is the willingness and determination to be as committed in the fourth quarter as we were at kick off. This applies to the fourth quarter of our lives, business year, or month; to hang in there with consistency of purpose to achieve the dreams of our lives. Oh, yes, we might have to change and modify these dreams but determination and persistence to go the distance are vital.

So often we give up so close to the realization of our dreams. Human nature so very often allows others to cause us to throw in the towel. Many times we get bogged down in the past rather than pursue the dreams of the future. Consider Paul's inspired wisdom as written in 2 Timothy,4:7.

"I have fought the good fight,

I have finished the course

I have kept the faith."

The relentless pursuit of a worthy ideal is how Earl Nightingale once described success.

When he was a child, Winston Churchill was almost totally rejected by indifferent parents. He wrote dozens of letters from his boarding school pleading with his mother to visit him at Christmas. The letters either went unanswered or the replies failed to refer to any plans about the family getting together at Christmas.

When all the other students left the school to be with their families during the holidays, young Winston remained alone at his school.

It is astounding that, with his incredibly unfortunate childhood – coupled with a series of failures at school and later political failure upon failure – that Winston Churchill would show such greatness in his country's finest hour.

But late in his life, he said something that gives us some insight into his greatness. He was 80 years old when he was asked to give the commencement address at Harrow, the boarding school he had attended as a youth. He stood up, looked out over his glasses at the young graduates and delivered one of the shortest commencement addresses on record.

"Never, never, never, never give up," he cried out.

With that, he sat down.

While at a lunch honouring Margaret Thatcher, former Iron Lady and British Prime Minister, she spoke about taking her country to war during the Falkland Islands crisis in 1982. She said you need three attributes:

1) the manpower and equipment

2) the ability to get the manpower and equipment to the arena of conflict

3) the resolve to win!

The resolve to win! Persistence! A never-give-up attitude! Hanging in when others turn away!

You are infinitely more capable of achieving almost any worthwhile goal/dream/objective with this one significant attribute: persistence.

———◆———

Every new opinion, at its
starting point, is precisely
in a minority of one.
—**Thomas Carlyle**

CHAPTER 31

What's Up With Norman?

ON JANUARY 7, 1995, I READ A STORY in the *Vancouver Sun* that has stuck with me ever since. It may have run in your paper.

Datelined Washington, D.C., it told of how Norman Vaughan had climbed a 3,140-metre mountain in Antarctica, less than 400 kilometres from the South Pole.

For anyone, it would have been a spectacular achievement. For Norman Vaughan, it was nothing short of a miracle. Norman was 89 years of age. Three days before the climb began, he had celebrated his birthday by blasting off 89 Fourth of July sparklers at base camp.

What really touched me was the quote at the beginning of the story. Six small words summed up Norman's life philosophy: "Dream big," he said, "and dare to fail."

What a great thought. "Dream big and dare to fail."

The Reuters story went on to say that Norman, a dog musher from Alaska, knew the truth of his advice. It took him more than 65 years, $1.5 million U.S. dollars, one failed attempt that ended in a plane crash and the loss of four favourite sled dogs who wandered away from the wreckage and were never found, and nine days of climbing to reach the peak named after him by polar explorer Admiral Richard Byrd. On his triumphant climb, he carried a stuffed toy husky to the summit in tribute to his dogs and to all Antarctic sled dogs "who never gave up."

Because of a fused ankle and a knee replacement, Norman had to climb the mountain straight up, using 7,128 footsteps hacked out of the ice with an axe by lead climber Vern Tejas.

On the windswept, frozen mountain, Norman read a message that dedicated the climb to Admiral Byrd and two Harvard roommates, the late Edward Goodale and Freddy Crockett. The three dropped out of school in 1928 and went to work as dog handlers for Byrd's 1928-30 Antarctic expedition.

Norman later told a news conference at the National Geographic Society in Washington, which helped sponsor the trip, that the birthday sparklers were a gift from his wife, fellow climber Carolyn Muegge-Vaughan. She had told him that the whole mountain was his birthday cake, that the snow was the frosting.

We all relish our personal triumphs from time to time, and so we should. But the achievement of Norman Vaughan was a triumph of monumental proportion that continues to inspire me, and perhaps will inspire *you.*

As important as it was for Norman to "dream big," it was just as important that he went in "daring to fail."

How often have you dreamed of achieving something you desperately wanted, then stopped before you started, believing it just wouldn't work out?

Everything we do involves *some* kind of risk. Rather than fear failure, we should train ourselves to take more risks, set our sights on higher mountains. We must detour more often from the comfortable, ordinary, familiar roads we travel too frequently. We need to shift into four-wheel-drive and discover the promising new territory that's over the unmapped horizon and, if we get lost, be prepared to find our way back.

Many people throughout history have told us in one way or another that if we're not doing *something,* we're doing *nothing.* People like Norman Vaughan motivate us to make the most of life, to set our sights on something we want and to go after it, even when the odds for success are against us.

If Norman Vaughan can come back at 89 from a fused ankle, a reworked knee and a failed first try to climb a frozen Antarctic mountain, that's more than enough to inspire *me* to get off my butt more often and get on with the pursuit of *my* dream – which involves risk, but great potential for reward.

I do have big dreams and, thankfully, they keep on coming. And you have big dreams that keep on coming. But too often we both cop out. We muddle around with mediocrity instead of going for the mountain.

"I've never told anyone about my big dream," we say to ourselves, "so for now I don't have to do anything about it. I'll do it next week. *Definitely* next week. I'll register for that course so my chances for success will be greater. I'll make that important call, start to map the plan. But right now, I deserve a break. Maybe a nap?"

Norman Vaughan's insistence on living life to the fullest helps to drive *me* to greater things. Every time I think of him trudging up all those frozen steps, I just can't permit myself to let life pass me by.

"Dream big dreams and dare to fail," he said.

And to celebrate that philosophy, light fireworks candles on a cake that's as big as a mountain!

Good for you, Norman. May you climb on to the stars!

CHAPTER 32

The Holy Grail For 150 Quid

I THINK MOST OF US HAVE SORT OF love-hate memories about the schools of our childhood. Some aspects about them were the stuff of the darkest nightmares. Others were quite wonderful – a collection of people and events that turned our lives in all the right directions.

I happen to remember Tavistock Hall in England's East Sussex with considerable affection. In many ways, it really was a turning point in my life and, as I shall soon relate, it taught me values that would stick with me forever.

When Raymond Ward, the principal of Tavistock Hall, wrote me in February of 1995 to invite me to the school's 50th reunion, I jumped at the chance, and bought a ticket for the event for £35. (I don't know why I mention that amount, but it's probably the equivalent of what it cost to be a boarder at the school for a term back in the '40s!) Remarkably, Ray Ward had kept track of 1,600 boys who had passed through the school over the years and I was on the list.

In July, I flew from Vancouver to London, rented a car, and headed south down familiar-yet-unfamiliar roads, through scenes of my childhood. Before checking into a nearby hotel, I went straight to Tavistock, first to make sure I could still find it, and second to soak up some of the '90s atmosphere prior to the party.

The sortie of discovery turned into two hours with the head-mistress – and the "head" following endless cups of tea. It was an afternoon that made me feel most welcome. That afternoon, Ray presented me with a picture of the "Fathers' Eleven," the cricket team of parents that included my own dad, when they played together while I was at school back in 1952. Good memories and a wonderful gift.

The reunion itself was a most pukka affair: Black tie, tents on the school lawns, caterers from the village, a band, 500 people – and me at the head table because I had journeyed the farthest! Surveying the scene, I soon discovered that, while some of the faculty were vaguely familiar, I really knew no one there. But it didn't really matter. It was good to be back and the old gang, quite predictably, had moved on.

Halfway through the dinner of roast beef, Yorkshire pudding, three veg and lots of gravy, the auction began that, along with part of the tab for the event, would raise funds for Tavistock Hall. There were several items that, while exciting, were really not for me. Living in Vancouver, I couldn't see how I could ever make use of two weeks in Cornwall or a trip for two to sunny Spain, even though both sounded mighty tempting.

But one thing *did* excite me. It was a book called *Be a Man,* written by one H. Bucknall back in 1917 as "a word in season to junior boys" who were in his care as principal of the Carlisle Preparatory School.

"Bucky" went on to become principal of *my* school and, even though the inside front cover showed that the book had been due back at the Tavistock School Library on February 6, 1948, it was now up for auction. It's amazing to what ends school libraries will go to get their just dues! (Bucky, regretfully, had died only a few months prior to the reunion, but his wife Ann, looking remarkably well, had come to the reunion along with several members of the family.)

But no matter how it got there, and more than any castles in Spain or windswept coasts in Cornwall, I wanted to have *Be a Man* for my very own.

Acting as auctioneer, the school custodian accepted my opening bid of £5 and, in short order, opposing bids of £10, £15, £20 and £25 followed. When I bid £150, reason seemed to rule and the custodian simply said: "I think we'll stop there." And the book was mine. A treasure from another age, the wisdom of a man who felt the urge to write "a word in season" to junior boys in the world of 1917.

Before the event was over, I had Ann Bucknall and as many of the Bucknall clan as I could find autograph the book.

All of them added to the value of something I knew I would treasure forever.

I began re-reading *Be a Man* on the long plane ride home and, despite its sometimes strange language (i.e., chapter heads like Coming Up to the Scratch, Facing Difficulties, Hardening Up) and philosophy, it really was a spellbinding read. I tried to visualize the period in which it was written. The First World War had already been tearing at the graduates of Bucky's school for three years. The headings of the book's 10 slim chapters would perhaps have steeled others for conflict.

When I finished reading the book somewhere high over Canada's Northwest Territories, I realized that Bucky had begun to sow new seeds of life for those boys in 1917 and, in 1946, when I first read *Be a Man,* he was doing the same for me.

Bucky was writing for an audience of pre-teenagers, but his rules for life are somehow universal. I can read and react to them now as I could as a pre-pubescent. Permit me to share some of his wisdom:

"The boy who doesn't now and then settle down to some serious occupation *of his own free will,* whether it is a matter of saying his prayers, reading a good book, or writing a careful letter, is neglecting a most important part of his self training," said Bucky, "and his whole character will suffer from that neglect. And don't forget that it is by your character that people will know and judge you, like or dislike you, help or hinder you."

Involvement in some kind of serious occupation, said Bucky, will add strength to a boy's character, and the tremendously important quality of determination to his will.

In order to grow, he said, muscles must have exercise. It's the same with the development of the mind. If you don't become a serious person – at the right time and in the right place – you will never be a man of the least importance or gain the respect of people whose opinion is worth anything.

"We are all agreed, I suppose, that it is the duty of everyone to try to be of use in the world – to try, by living honourable, straightforward, unselfish lives, to benefit other people. Only in this way can we do what we are here to do – that is, leave the world a little better for our having lived in it.

". . . Our motives for doing right improve with our conduct."

Bucky concluded his first chapter: "It isn't good enough to live nobly because you want people to say you are a noble man. But to live nobly because you love what is noble and hate what is base, and because you wish to do good in the world by force of a noble example, that *is* good enough. Nothing, in fact, could be better."

Bucky said that it takes time to get really interested in something, adding that, "I believe there are thousands and thousands of men in England dragging out a dull and uninterested existence simply and solely because they could never persevere with anything long enough to get interested in it."

When famous men were boys, he said, they didn't *know* they were going to be famous. They became famous because *when* they were boys they exercised their brains, persevered with their lessons and were never content to be left behind.

Bucky devoted a long chapter on "being straight," as in honest, in which he discussed the unforgivable sins of lying and cheating.

" . . . a boy who is so careless about his honour as to cheat is, very often, careless enough to tell lies about it, and then, of course, you immediately have that disagreeable combination, a liar *and* a cheat, both of them hideously ugly words to apply to an English boy."

Bad habits, said Bucky, begin at a tender age. "The habits you form during your boyhood are liable to cling to you all your life, and you have to be a very strong-minded sort of chap to be able to break yourself of them."

Boys, he said, can roughly be divided into two classes: those who have a code of honour, and those who have not.

"By a code of honour I don't mean a certain number of rules which they have learnt by heart . . . but certain fairly distinct notions of what is right and wrong, and an ever-growing inclination to stick to the former and avoid the latter. . . One thing a boy *must* have is a code of honour. He gets it by deciding for himself very definitely what are the things to do and what are the things to avoid doing."

Bucky said that patterns of dishonesty are deep rooted:

"We are apt to think that the piece of dishonesty for which a man, especially a man in a good position, is ruined, is the first wrong he ever did . . . As a rule, he has been doing wrong and foolish things for years, and this last thing is only a trifle more wrong and more foolish than lots of other things he has done, and had, besides, the supreme disadvantage of being discovered."

On facing difficulties, Bucky said that in many cases courage, like most other qualities, has to be cultivated. If you want to be brave, he said "the first thing to do is to put your house in order – that is, get your code of honour working vigorously, and tune up your daily life to a higher standard of effort."

He said that willpower is a faculty we all possess, and it too can be developed by exercise.

" . . . allow yourself to develop into a coward while you are a boy, you will be a coward when you are a man. You need courage nearly every day that dawns, and if you haven't got it you will lead the life of a valet." (I apologize to all honourable valets, but these are Bucky's words and this was 1917!)

"Live a hard, laborious life, tramp the country, take up boxing, take up fencing, throw yourself heart and soul into your football, into your cricket, your swimming, diving, wrestling, and anything else that will brace the nerves and increase your stamina.

"Learn to depend on yourself. Teach yourself to be brave. A brave boy is one of the finest things on God's earth."

Bucky's physical standards became tougher in his "Hardening Up" chapter when he began to talk at length of the benefits of, among other things, cold baths. I can't ever recall taking this piece of advice.

"If you want to be fitter than you are; if you want to brace up your nerves; if you want to harden up your system; if you want to enjoy your meals more, and add a daily pleasure to your lives, start cold baths in the morning," he said, "but start 'em carefully."

What about when you're not making it and you want to give up? Bucky covered that too.

"Important as it is that you should master your difficulties, it is more important still that you should go on trying. The boy who gives up trying because he does not succeed is, without knowing it, throwing away a chance of being successful in another direction."

Bucky told a story about a boy who seemed to fail in just about every class, except geography:

" . . . He began to read books of travel and exploration; he used to make maps and plans of the neighbourhood . . . He went on and on, getting keener and keener, reading more books, making more maps, until at length it became clear that he was remarkably clever – at his geography – and I can tell you now that Harry, who is no longer a boy, is well known as a brave and adventurous explorer."

Bucky figured there are hundreds, if not thousands, of "thick" boys who never discover their strong subjects because they give up trying to compete with clever boys.

"Plod along, my thick young friends," said the generous Bucky, "and don't give up."

It's important, said Bucky, to "play the game," to do things fairly and squarely, to be a good sport.

"The sporting boy shows his superiority to the unsporting boy in a thousand little ways. He would rather take a flogging than cause anyone else to get one. He would rather bite off his tongue than turn in a sneak. He would rather lose a goal than get one by unfair means. He would rather fight a boy his own size than a boy much smaller than himself."

Bucky considered it most important to guard the mind against most anything likely to infect it.

"Crazes," he said, "are terribly infectious. It only needs one boy to bring a water-pistol or a new kind of stink bomb to school to start a hundred other boys doing the same thing. In fact, there ought to be a law that any boy suspected of the intention of starting a new craze (or re-starting an old one) should be sent to a hospital for infectious diseases of the mind. He would be cured of water-pistolitis by having to shoot at a dummy schoolboy (or, better still, a waxwork figure of his former master) until he was absolutely fed up with it. If it happened to be stink-bombitis, he would be forced to smell his own stink-bombs for a week."

Minds must be protected from permanent injury, said Bucky.

"Great rewards await those who keep out of their minds everything that is ugly and useless and only let in things that are beautiful and useful."

Go for the good things, he said, "you will not only find that you are rapidly ceasing to care for poor things, but that your appreciation of good things is rapidly growing."

Thoughtfulness for others counted large for Bucky:

" . . . your simple duty is to avoid doing or saying unkind things, and to lend a helping and protecting hand when it is plainly needed.

"When you are a man you will have great need of a particular quality which is calculated not only to make your own life smoother and happier but the lives of those around you smoother and happier too. This is the quality of kindliness. The man who has no kindliness in him cannot be a happy man, because he will live in a world made up of people he doesn't like and who don't like him."

Bucky said that all this begins in childhood.

"Instead of getting into the senseless habit of saying and doing unkind and thoughtless things, (these children) got into the sensible habit of saying or doing kind and thoughtful things. Unknown to them, they were forming the habit of controlling their tongues . . . and sowing the seeds of kindliness and wisdom.

"If you are ever going to win the love and respect of those around you, you must teach yourself to think more of other people than of yourself . . . unselfish people form a habit of wanting only those things that are of real worth, such as wisdom and contentment and other noble qualities. Selfish people strive perpetually after pleasures that fade and possessions which will add nothing to the treasures of the world or the happiness of mankind.

"The world is full of goodness for those who are good. For the kind, the world is full of kindness. For the unselfish, the world is full of unselfishness.

"If you wish people to be kind to you, you must be kind to them, and if you wish people to be generous to you, you must be generous to them. The kindness and generosity you show to others will nearly always bring you kindness and generosity in return."

Robert Fulghum wrote a bestseller called *All I Really Need to Know I Learned in Kindergarten*. Wisdom, he said, was not at the top of the graduate-school mountain, but there in the sandpile at Sunday School.

Perhaps much of what *I* needed to know, I learned at the feet of Bucky Bucknall. It was learning to love cold baths and to take headers off the high board, but, as I learned in his book, it was much more than that.

I may not have known it back then, but I would take Bucky's lessons with me through life. They would become good guides for business, for building a family, being a husband and father. They would be the beginnings of speeches that I make today and will continue making tomorrow. And they are the stuff of books.

I'm glad the custodian halted the bidding in such a sporting manner. I got to take home the Holy Grail for 150 quid!

As a postscript to this event, I recall sitting and reminiscing with many people that evening. At one point, I remarked that it was a shame that there existed no original photograph of Tavistock Hall. The woman next to me, Juliet Murray, piped up, "I'd be happy to paint an original of the hall for £400." I had no idea she was a well-known local artist. I casually agreed that would be a great idea. And then I promptly forgot about the conversation.

Two months later, a package arrived at my office from England. I tore open the wrapping and stood gaping at an original, beautifully painted image of Tavistock Hall. Now my memories of those special years are crystalized in living color – and hang on the walls of my den.

Lord Kelvin was President of England's Royal Society from 1890 to 1895. Britons listened attentively when the Lord made three predictions:

1. Radio has no future

2. Heavier-than-air flying machines are impossible

3. X-rays are a hoax

CHAPTER 33

The Road Not Taken

ENGELBERT HUMPERDINCK, FAMOUS FOR hits like *Please Release Me* and *After the Loving,* didn't always have that name. Born Arnold George Dorsey in Madras, India, he called himself Gerry Dorsey when he first hit it big in the '50s. Despite being easier to spell, he switched to Engelbert Humperdinck.

I never asked Engelbert exactly why he changed his name to match that of the 19th-century German composer of the opera *Hansel and Gretel.* I can only presume he wanted to stand out in the crowd and Engelbert Humperdinck was considerably more memorable in the competitive world of public performance than Arnold or Gerry Dorsey.

For a brief time in my showbiz career, I worked with "Engy," as we called him, and had things turned out differently, I might have worked with him for a lot longer in a whole other career.

All of these memories were stirred by a piece I read in the *Vancouver Sun* in late October 1995. Writer John Armstrong told the story of a singer named Ilene Woods whose life was changed when she became the voice of Walt Disney's *Cinderella*.

In 1947, John wrote, two hopeful songwriters were pitching their work for a new Disney cartoon project and they enlisted Ilene, newly arrived in Los Angeles, to sing some new songs on a demonstration recording. The studio had already auditioned 350 actresses for the part without finding one that met Walt's requirements for the singing voice of Cinderella.

"I'd known (songwriters) Mack David and Hal Livingstone in New York," said Ilene, "and they asked me to go into the studio with a piano to record *A Dream is a Wish Your Heart Makes, So This is Love* and *Bibbidi-Bobbidi-Boo*. He (Walt) bought the songs and hired me, too. I was the only leading lady he ever used that had just a regular, natural 'popular' voice."

My situation wasn't much different. It was back in the 1960s and I had come to Canada to build a career as a comedian, which I found tougher than I had expected. Let's face it, I was often close to broke. But my fortunes soon changed. In exchange for free passage, I was hired to be the funny man on a cruise ship from Vancouver, through the Panama Canal, and back to England. I snapped it up.

England was kinder then than Vancouver had been. I soon began picking up work on the circuit, entertaining in venues that ran the gamut from the grungiest of pubs to the toniest of hotels, to a club like Playboy, to a show of my own on British television.

Somewhere along the way, a producer heard and saw me and decided that the international flavour of my material – and the U.K.-North American lilt to my dialect – could be a salable product not just in Britain, but also in the United States.

I was signed to host a pilot for ABC Television, with stars like Engelbert Humperdinck, Tom Jones, José Feliciano and Barbara Eden of *I Dream of Jeannie* fame. ITV would tape it.

I remember the running gag we had on the show, which, in retrospect, was pretty lame stuff. We would take a film crew all over London and ask a variety of people the question: "Where are the men's toilets?" The responses, of course, were quite varied: "Up those stairs and turn right;" "I haven't a clue;" "You got me, guv;" and so on. When it came time to tape the show, we edited the best answers in with completely different questions.

"Have you ever heard of Engelbert Humperdinck?" got the response: "You got me, guv." "Where's the best place in London to find Engelbert Humperdinck?" answered: "Up those stairs and turn right." You get the picture.

Anyway, Engelbert and Tom sang and José played and Barbara looked beautiful and I kept it all together with the funny stuff and, in short order, the pilot was in the can and off to ABC.

Despite the fun times and rosy future, I had reached a turning point in my life. While things may have seemed fine, I was feeling the need for change. Life as a comedian upon the wicked stage, while I loved the adulation, wasn't something that I had visualized as a lifelong pursuit. Something else seemed to be pulling me in other directions.

Canada was one of them. Despite the unevenness of my earlier life there, I wanted to go back. It felt much more like home than England did and I was prepared to return to take it on one more time.

At about the same time the first Engelbert show landed in New York, I had landed in Vancouver. Almost immediately I was picked up by old friend Ken Stauffer to be the opening act at his Cave theatre-restaurant for the Mills Brothers. They were always a sell-out and the audiences were responsive not just to them, but to the whole package, and that included me as a warm-up.

As I was about to open for my first gig at the Cave, I learned from my agent that Engelbert's pilot had worked like a darn and they wanted to sign me up for the season.

It was decision time.

I had enjoyed my time in England, but I was ready to leave. I had been accepted quickly in Vancouver and could obviously hold my own while I searched for whatever it was I was looking for. Engelbert had been a kick and there was obviously a future for me, probably in places like New York, Las Vegas and wherever that lifestyle would take me.

I said no.

Looking back on a life that would lead to publishing and motivational speaking, I have no doubt at all that I made the right decision. There was a choice of two doors and, following my head and not my heart, I walked through one of them because I felt that, one step at a time, I was moving in the direction I wanted to go.

It was great telling jokes back in those days, hearing the laughter come back. It's been much better since, knowing that once I found my niche, I had infinitely more belief in myself and in the consistency of my purpose.

I still tell jokes. I *love* to tell jokes and I know that their inclusion in my presentations has helped me immeasurably to gain the distinction I now enjoy in the competitive world of public speaking. My "dues" were paid in some grisly spots, but I will never regret all that learning.

The key to happiness, as I've often said, is having dreams. The key to success is making them come true. In almost every speech I make, I refer to the three "Ps" that are central to my life: persistence, patience and positive attitude.

Clearly you need more than just these traits of character to achieve any level of success, but without them the climb to the mountaintop is all but impossible, and the dreams quickly fade.

If you look around your community and identify someone you view as having "made it" in every respect, remember that the process was never automatic. They climbed their mountain one step at a time. Persistence and perseverance were the driving forces behind their dreams and when they slipped, positive attitude helped them begin again.

Thomas Edison, who we remember for his inventive brilliance, said that genius is made up of 10 per cent inspiration and 90 per cent perspiration. Once you've found your path, as I eventually did, it takes a ton of work to keep the dream unfolding.

Every great achiever we've ever known began with a dream.

Columbus, Martin Luther King Jr., Abraham Lincoln, the builders behind the super-sonic Concorde – this book is not big enough to name them all – began with a dream, a vision, an idea.

"How would it be if . . ?"

"If we were to take this and move it over here and take this and move it over here . . . There, *now* it works!"

Norman Vincent Peale built an entire life encouraging millions of men and women around the world to pursue their dreams. He said: "If you have an idea, if you have a dream, if you have a vision, do it, do it now. Don't die with the music still in you."

You can always feel it coming. Don't be sidetracked by short-term satisfaction. Choose *your* path and stay on it. "If it has to be, then it's up to me." Those who have lived their dreams have said it again and again.

Until you make a commitment to your dream, it will be nothing more than a fantasy – and no fantasy of mine has ever come true. Don't wait.

Henry Ford said you can't build a reputation on what you're *going* to do. You have to do it. As I have said elsewhere in this book, you succeed when you do it right, you learn when you do it wrong, you fail if you do nothing. Doing nothing is the worst sin of all.

I apologize for quoting too often the thoughts of others, but they say it so *well*. Like Henry David Thoreau, who said if you advance with confidence in the direction of your dreams and endeavour to live the life that you have imagined, you will meet with a success unexpected in common hours. You will put some things behind you and you will pass through an invisible boundary to a state where new universal and more liberal laws will begin to establish themselves around and within you.

I can assure you that Mr. Thoreau is absolutely correct. The rewards are there. If not this way, *which* way? If not now, *when?* If not you, *who?*

Many people fail because they believe the adage, "If you don't succeed, try something else." I say that, in most cases, that doesn't work. People succeed and dreams come true because they stay the course and follow the true direction.

Dreams require courage, determination and sacrifice. In hockey language, you need to be as committed to your dreams at the end of the third period as you were at the opening face-off.

One more quote, this time from author Berton Braley, who said: "If you want a thing bad enough to go out and fight for it, to work day and night for it, to give your time, your peace and sleep for it; if all that you dream and scheme is about it and life seems useless and worthless without it; if you gladly sweat for it and fret for it and lose all your terror of the opposition for it; if you simply go after that thing you want with all of your capacity, strength and tenacity, faith, hope and confidence and stern pertinacity; if neither cold, poverty, famine, nor gout, sickness, nor pain of the body and brain can keep you away from the thing that you want; if dogged and grim you beseech and best it, with the help of God, you *will* get it."

I have always believed that the choices we make end up controlling the chooser. Throughout our entire life we will be faced with literally thousands of decisions that may very well have a huge impact on our lives; decisions that may alter the destiny that awaits us.

The Engelbert Humperdinck decision was not an easy one to make – potential stardom, being linked with one of the world's foremost entertainers. But something told me it was not right to go back to London and fulfil that dream. Another would take its place. You see, sometimes we need to change direction, but that doesn't mean giving up on our dreams. My time was yet to come. The decision to do Engelbert's television show was not the right path at the right time. My instincts told me as much. So I turned down this unique opportunity, with no regrets. God had other dreams for me to choose from and the desires of my heart were yet to be realized.

I liked *Cinderella*. I liked *A Wish is a Dream Your Heart Makes*. Even more, I treasure the dreams that, for me, continue to keep coming true.

Remember that, sometimes, perhaps quite *often*, new bright and shiny lures look right and you're tempted, oh *so* tempted, to bite. Search your soul. Try to get outside of yourself and look back in. Weigh your decision with great care. It works today. How about tomorrow? Do you get on the plane and fly now or do you say no, I'm taking a different road.

I did, and I have no regrets.

And wherever *you* are Engy, break a leg!

CHAPTER 34

Cancer Is So Limited

I DON'T HAVE EXACT STATISTICS at hand, but I'm always amazed at how many people have had, or continue to be afflicted by, cancer.

Anyone who has read my second book, *You Can if You Believe You Can,* will know that it struck *me* for a while and, I suppose, was a catalyst for many changes in my life.

Because I was a victim of cancer and because many people know about it through my book and my public appearances, I also meet and speak one-on-one to others who have been touched in one way or another by some form of cancer.

My biggest message to all of these people is one of hope.

While I still go to the cancer clinic in Vancouver every three months for x-rays, blood tests and a head-to-toe examination, I believe that I have completely recovered – and I go about my business and my life with a presumption that I am as fit and maybe even fitter than I was before it happened.

One thing that keeps me strong and smiling is the support that I receive from many, many people. Some I know, but many are complete strangers. I have received hundreds of cards, letters, poems and other expressions that have all been very touching and much appreciated. Quite often, from people who are miles and even continents apart, I receive the same message.

The following has come from more than 50 people, and if you would be so kind as to keep passing it on, it will lift the spirits of many, many more. I have no idea who may have written it. I only know that I believe every word of it.

Cancer is so limited . . .
It cannot cripple love,
It cannot shatter hope,
It cannot corrode faith,
It cannot destroy peace,
It cannot kill friendship, .
It cannot suppress memories,
It cannot silence courage,
It cannot invade the soul,
It cannot steal eternal life,
It cannot conquer the Spirit.

CHAPTER 35

A Place to Turn Off the Noise

SOMETIMES IN MY TRAVELS I seek solace from the rush by going to church. Anywhere in the world, the embracing arms of a church and the people within it can turn off the noise – no matter how you may define it – and turn on welcoming taps of calm.

On assignment in the historic city of Boston in the spring of 1995, I went to Trinity Church, founded on October 17, 1733 – before the *country* was founded.

According to the brochure that I snaffled after the morning service, Trinity, of Episcopal persuasion, first occupied an unpretentious structure at the corner of Summer Street and Bishop's Alley (now Hawley Street), surrounded by fine residences and gardens. In 1929 a larger, dignified stone Gothic Revival building was erected on the same site and it was here that Phillips Brooks came as rector in 1869. Many years later he was appointed the ninth rector of Trinity Church and the sixth bishop of Massachusetts.

Summer Street by then was a business centre. Under Mr. Brooks' urging, the present location on Copley Square in the newly developed Black Bay area was purchased in January 1872. Henry Hobson Richardson was chosen architect and plans were under way when the old structure was destroyed in the Boston Fire of November 8 and 9, 1872.

The new Trinity Church, consecrated on February 9, 1877, is now considered by many to be the masterpiece of church architecture in America. It really is a wonderful building and I urge you, no matter what your religious beliefs, to visit Trinity Church if ever you're in Boston.

As well as the lift that First Trinity gave me with its architecture, the welcome of its people and the message I took away from the morning service, it also gave me a snippet of new knowledge. Phillips Brooks originally was not a religious man but had decided to travel to the Holy Land. He was a 300-pound man who sat on a hill overlooking Bethlehem. As he gazed upon this little, insignificant town not far from Jerusalem, he was moved to write one of the world's most beloved Christmas carols – *O Little Town of Bethlehem*. I'm sure that every Bostonian probably knows this, but it was news to me and it was information that has stuck with me ever since.

Mr. Brooks' organist, Lewis Redner, who was professionally a highly successful real estate broker and on Sundays a leader in the Sunday School, set Mr. Brooks' words to music for the church's children's choir. *O Little Town of Bethlehem* was subsequently sung by choirs and people like me around the world.

> *O little town of Bethlehem, How still we see thee lie;*
> *Above thy deep and dreamless sleep, the silent stars go by.*
> *Yet in thy dark streets shineth the everlasting light;*
> *The hopes and fears of all the years are met in thee tonight.*

Mr. Brooks was moved to write his words and my only purpose now is to tell you his story. Because of it, I am linked forever not only to Trinity Church, but also to Boston.

My continuing belief is that our world, in all of its fascinating detail, is here to discover. And in every corner, there's invariably a pleasant surprise.

As you share Christmas Eve and Day with your family and friends and contemplate your own fears and, more important, your hopes for the future, consider the incredible event that changed the world forever. This magnificent night some 2,000 years ago.

*If you could give your son
or daughter only one gift,
let it be enthusiasm*

—**Unknown**

CHAPTER 36

A Family Like Mine

SUCCESS IS ALL THE SWEETER when shared with a loving family.

I'm reminded of a scene in Dickens' *A Christmas Carol.* The Ghost of Christmas Yet to Come has taken Ebenezer Scrooge to watch his household staff sell off the clothes and furnishings they had stolen from the room where Scrooge had died alone. It was a priceless scene, but at the same time it was terribly sad. Scrooge, at the end of a miserable life, had slipped into the next life, "as solitary as an oyster." Friendless in life, there were none to mourn him at death. Those who had served him remained to rob him. It was perhaps that vision, more than any other, that convinced Scrooge to change his ways.

Thankfully, our family has never had to learn hard lessons from spirits that come in the night. Kay and I and our three girls have had our moments, but we've been able to overcome difficulties. Today I think we're as good as families get and I'm completely aware of the importance each member plays in the success that I enjoy. My family is integral to absolutely everything I do and the significance of this is never taken for granted.

At the end of 1995, round about the time Scrooge was getting its first television airing of the holiday season, our family got together for one of its irregular "meetings," times when we take stock of where we are, how we're doing, where we're going, what needs fixing, what's good and not so good about the lives we are leading together.

I think these kinds of sessions are most valuable, especially with the crazy lives many of us lead these days. Without knowing it, we can spin off into another world and our poor family too often gets short shrift. We wake up one day to chaos that might have been prevented, to all kinds of problems that might not have happened if only we had kept the lines of communication open.

The fireplace that is family needs frequent stoking!

As part of our meeting, and because my life is as hectic as lives get, I asked Kay, Rebecca, Samantha and Amanda how I've been doing as a husband and father. Thankfully, my scorecard, made up of a lot of little and big things, was in great shape. Let me tell you about some of the things that are important to my family. They are not in any particular order.

- My family loves the fact that when they call me at the office, their calls, no matter what I'm doing at the time, go right through. (I subsequently learned that there's a note at the switchboard desk that outlines this precise instruction to anyone who may be on duty there.)

- My family loves the fact that we take regular holidays together. Samantha is now 25, Rebecca is 21 and Amanda is 19 and once every year, sometimes more often, we blast off to a vacation spot together. When we get there, we do things *together.* Unbelievable family nourishment.

- As well as taking holidays together, we maintain similar bonds when we're in town. We go out for dinner, to hockey games, plays and shows as a *family.* Another positive.

- My family is appreciative of the fact that I call and let them know if I'm going to be late arriving home from the office. A little thing that can stop a potential problem in its tracks.

- They like the fact that I find the time to do things for them – to run special errands, organize breakfast, leave nutty notes on the fridge, phone from the car for no reason at all, laugh, cry, have fun.

- They like it when I listen to them. If I'm running too hard and they say it's time to slow down and I do, they like that. And so does my body!

- We shop together at Christmastime, as we did over the years for back to school. Important family activity.

- They are grateful that when I'm on the road, they know how to reach me, that my schedule and phone numbers are always available. They like phone calls from out of town.

- Kay enjoys our weekly dates, just us. In the summer months, it's 18 holes of golf followed by dinner.

- Several times each year, the girls come along on my speaking tours and assist with book sales and other meaningful responsibilities on the road. More bonding . . . and the experience of travel and education.

- Over the years, we have tried snow skiing, jet skiing, water skiing, horseback riding, golfing, parasailing, swimming, snorkelling, moped riding in Bermuda, tennis – we have discovered that families that play together indeed stay together.

Add all of this up and it is no more or less than it really should be. Families and careers come apart at the seams because too often it may seem easier to take a selfish route, to let the good stuff slip, to forget that it's with the family that most everything really begins.

It's more than coincidence that strongly knit families foster careers that succeed.

I'm from a generation that taught me that I have a responsibility to my mate and my children. I have to work hard at relationships, at parenting. I have to come through when it counts. I can't let my family down. I can't say I will do something and not do it.

In June 1994, I was invited to speak at a conference in Tucson, Arizona. The conference was being held the day before Kay and I were due to be in Vancouver at the graduation dinner for our youngest daughter Amanda. We had never been invited to one of these dinners and it was extremely important to Amanda that we attend.

I was to make the speech in Tucson on a Friday. Amanda's dinner was scheduled for Vancouver on Saturday night. There would be lots of time to fulfil the assignment and be back for the dinner.

I made the speech on Friday afternoon, returned to my room and packed. There would be a wakeup call at 5 a.m., I would take a limo to the airport, catch a 7 a.m. United Airlines flight to Los Angeles, connect with a 12:40 flight to Vancouver and be home in time to shower, change and head off with Kay for Amanda's big night.

Next morning, I checked in at Tucson, got my boarding pass and waited in the lounge for the 7 a.m. departure. At 6:45, an efficient member of United's ground staff walked over to advise me that my flight, due in from Dallas, had been delayed by bad weather. No problem, I said, I'll take the next flight.

Next flight? The next flight would not leave until mid-afternoon. There was no way I would make the Los Angeles connection to Vancouver.

I tried every commercial airline possible and came up empty. What's a dad to do? I had made a promise. Amanda would be waiting. Kay would be waiting. If I *didn't* make it, there would be no doubt they would understand. Storms in Dallas really had nothing to do with me. But if I *did* make it?

I hit the Yellow Pages. Yes, a private jet was available. Yes, it could get me to Los Angeles in time to make the connection. Yes, it would cost me more than the fee I had made for the previous afternoon's speech. Yes, I would be with Kay at Amanda's dinner.

I rented the jet. As we climbed out of Tucson into the clear

Arizona sky, I felt good indeed. Empty wallet? Sure, but I'd never felt better in my life.

Another story:

When Rebecca was in Grade Six, she had a dream of being fluent in English and French. For a Canadian kid, it was a pretty good dream. After all, Canada's official languages *are* English and French.

Through primary school, junior and senior high, Rebecca was taught entirely in French and, through her good efforts, she became, and remains, bilingual. (I remember that quite early, she conversed in French to her friends on the phone. Kay and I, who remain unilingually rooted in English, didn't have a clue what she was talking about!)

During her first year at Simon Fraser University in Vancouver, Rebecca had the urge to continue her education and her French immersion in France. Together we chose a university in Nice with Canadian links. In the summer prior to her departure she worked to help with the burden of what would be substantially greater expense – certainly much more than an easy daily commute to Simon Fraser!

Even though we had always spent our holidays together as a family, and had travelled all over the place, Rebecca had never lived away from home. There was no question that the flight to London and on to France and the long time away from home that would follow, would be daunting.

In September 1994, I took her to the airport in Vancouver for the continuation of her life adventure. With just 25 minutes to go

before the British Airways flight left for London, I said to Rebecca, "It's time, kiddo." I knew where the gate was, how long it
would take her to get through security and onto the plane.

She paused for a moment, then in front of everyone, dropped
her knapsack, threw her arms around my neck and said: "Dad, I
love you so much. I'm scared to death. I don't want to go!"

But she *did* go. Her dream was still happening.

A few weeks earlier, probably anticipating that the early
stages of life in Nice would be anything but nice, Rebecca had
convinced me to somehow arrange a speaking assignment or
other business meeting in London around the end of November. It
would be great, she said. I could fly her up from the south of
France and we could spend a weekend together.

Being a sucker of a dad, but more so because I loved her, I
figured it would be a great idea. The lobby of the Grosvenor, I
said. It's a promise.

At the time, I had absolutely no idea how I might get to London, but being perpetually positive and always believing that you
really can do what you think about most of the time, I started to
think of almost nothing else but how to get to London in late
November, hopefully for the lowest cost, and, ideally, at no cost.

Within a few weeks, I had secured a speaking engagement in
the Bahamas, which would take place on the weekend prior to the
projected London date. That assignment would be followed by an
engagement in New York, just two days ahead of the London
weekend. Hey, except for the Atlantic crossing, I was *there*!

I took the plunge and booked a ticket from New York to

London. Rebecca would fly from Nice, we would have a great weekend and I would keep my promise as a dad. Rebecca, of course, never *doubted* that it would happen.

Then I thought to myself: "That was pretty easy. Now how can I make this thing even better?"

I had accumulated points on another airline so I said to my wife Kay and our daughters Samantha and Amanda: "Why don't you take a few days off and fly to London to surprise the heck out of Rebecca?" They didn't take much convincing. What are memories made of, anyway?

But part of our family's success is good communication, and while everybody dearly wanted to go to London, Kay and Amanda were going into finals at university and reluctantly had to decline. I would wing in from New York, and only Samantha would fly over the Pole from Vancouver. We would meet at the Grosvenor a few hours before Rebecca arrived from Nice. What had started as a fun weekend would still go right over the top, despite having to leave Kay and Amanda to their exams!

But there would be more.

Being as adventurous as we are, I arranged with Anna Ponur, the guest relations manager at the Grosvenor House on Park Lane, to have Samantha hidden behind the check-in counter. Just as Rebecca was signing in, she would leap out and scream: "Surprise!"

At 7:30, as Sam was preparing to get herself into position and I was pacing the Grosvenor House lobby, a cab pulled up at the front and out stepped Rebecca.

If the Vancouver airport departure in September had been one filled with sadness, this was a moment of pure happiness. They say that hearts leap, and mine certainly did that night. We ran to greet each other, hugged hard and cried tears of joy.

We talked beside the cab. I told Rebecca that I had arranged for her to have her own room and that she would have to check in herself. We went inside and began to walk toward the registration desk.

Sam, meanwhile, was in the back room getting ready to play her role, and as she stood there waiting, the hotel manager walked into the room. Seeing Sam, an obvious stranger among the cash, the accounts receivable and other documents, he quite rightly asked who she was and what was she doing in the hotel's very private space?

At this point, guest relations manager Anna jumped in, explaining that the guy coming toward the counter was the "intruder's" father and the girl next to him was the "intruder's" sister. The father was from Vancouver, the sister was from Nice, they hadn't seen each other for a while and what was about to happen would end up in a delightful family reunion. A bright guy, the manager picked up on the scheme in a second.

Turning to one of the hotel employees, he asked her to slip out of her Grosvenor House uniform jacket and pillbox hat and give it to Sam. The event was beginning to have all of the elements of a French farce, mixed nicely with a ridiculous British edge.

Sam, now in Grosvenor uniform, bow tie and hat, walked calmly to the desk as Rebecca, head down, was signing in.

"May I have your passport, please?" said Sam in a finely concocted British accent.

Rebecca looked up, fumbled for her passport, looked up, fumbled again, then realized in a spectacular instant that the pillbox-hatted person behind the counter was her sister Samantha.

The small crowd that had now gathered and was onto the act cheered wildly. Oblivious to the crowd, the Legge family threesome came together in a hug. As we walked away to the tea room, I saw two men, a woman and guest relations manager Anna wiping tears from their eyes. Magic times can happen anywhere.

I got a letter from Rebecca and it read:

"I'm not sure where to begin when I think of the incredible things that you have done for me. Being away for such a long time has shown me how much I appreciate you not only as a father, but as a friend. Your constant love and support have helped to keep me strong and my spirits high. Not a day goes by that I don't think about the way you make me laugh and smile. I miss so many things that I hadn't realized were so important to me – your cheerful disposition, your words of wisdom, your unconditional love. You are the most amazing father and I couldn't ask for anything more.

Thank you for everything. I love you

Bec"

As I said at the beginning, success is sweeter when shared with a loving family.

A family like mine.

CHAPTER 37

Food For Thought

I'VE BEEN ASKED ON SEVERAL OCCASIONS how books like this come together. What gets them started? Is there a beginning to the process, a middle and an end?

Books, while possessing a certain magic when they're done, really are like most projects that we take on in life. We feel driven to do something, so we do it. Books are written.

It seems like – and it *is* – years since I first thought that a book would be a good idea. So, in 1991, I called an old friend who makes his living as a writer and asked him if he would like to work with me on a book. I called him because I'm a much better speaker than a writer. I have the ideas and I enjoy plunking away at the first draft, but my spelling is atrocious and I really don't have what it takes to put one right word after another to create the good stuff that makes readable books.

Duncan Holmes and I met to talk about the first book in a restaurant called Dario's La Piazza Ristorante on Slocan Street, in Vancouver's Italian Cultural Centre. Despite the fact that its profile is lower than many of Vancouver's best restaurants, Dario's is a treasure of a place that serves fabulous food in surroundings that delight, with a style that is invariably pleasing.

Duncan and I met for lunch and Roberto served us. I know it sounds strange, but despite the fact that I must have had hundreds of lunches at Dario's over the years, I have no idea what Roberto's last name is. I know him and love him only as Roberto and that's the way it will stay.

Roberto is the kind of guy who takes your order without a pad, has complete command of the language of good food, can describe the luncheon special in always-tempting detail, presents the wine with flair, tops up the glasses, is unobtrusive in the maintenance of the meal, and magically arrives to attend his guests in every moment where there may be need.

Roberto was pleased that we were talking about a book right there in his restaurant and, as the words began to flow after many long and delightful lunches, he knew our purpose well and encouraged the book-building process on every lunch occasion.

When *How to Soar With the Eagles* was published in 1992, Roberto was delighted. We presented him with a copy and, as we began our second book, he was able to quote all kinds of "Eagles" philosophy and content. When *You Can if You Believe*

You Can came out in 1995, we gravitated again to Dario's to celebrate its release.

The books really have evolved over many lunches, all initiated for a purpose. My public speaking career continues, my anecdotal material accumulates, I progressively file it, and Duncan and I meet to transfer information. He takes my notes and augments them with notes of his own that can be used to add sensual flavour.

His questions are often about the simplest of things: "Was it raining?" "What were you wearing?" "Did you race to the plane?" Books are just words, but words can also paint pictures.

The right writer can get inside your head and quickly understand what it is you are trying to say. It may sound strange, but Duncan and I often talk more about the food, wine and other things than we do about where we're at with the book. But the stories and chapters build and there's always something new that we can talk and write about.

It was right at Dario's that I discovered the amazing piece of writing that follows and decided to include it in *this* book. It was the focus of a poster that had been published by American Arts and Graphics and was written by Wanda Hope Carter. I tried on several occasions to talk to American Arts to learn more about the poster and about Ms. Carter, but so far I have been unsuccessful.

Like much of the philosophy that gets into my presentations and books, the words and thoughts in this piece are incredibly simple, but in their simplicity they are also incredibly powerful.

To Achieve Your Dreams, said the title, Remember Your ABCs. And this is what Wanda Hope Carter wrote:

Avoid negative sources, people, places, things and habits.

Believe in yourself.

Consider things from every angle.

Don't give up and don't give in.

Enjoy life today, yesterday is gone, tomorrow may never come.

Family and friends are hidden treasures, seek them and enjoy their riches.

Give more than you planned to.

Hang on to your dreams.

Ignore those who try to discourage you.

Just do it.

Keep trying no matter how hard it seems, it will get easier.

Love yourself first and most.

Make it happen.

Never lie, cheat or steal, always strike a fair deal.

Open your eyes and see things as they really are.

Practice makes perfect.

Quitters never win and winners never quit.

Read, study and learn about everything important in your life.

Stop procrastinating.

Take control of your own destiny.

Understand yourself in order to better understand others.

Visualize it.

Want it more than anything.

Xcellerate your efforts.

You are unique in all God's creations, nothing can replace YOU.

Zero in on your target and go for it.

If you're looking for a guaranteed great lunch – or dinner – in Vancouver, consider Dario's. It's a great place to start a book, to start absolutely anything.

———◆———

There is little difference in people but the real difference makes a big difference. The little difference is attitude. The big difference is whether it is positive or negative.
—**W. Clement Stone**

CHAPTER 38

Stop Me if You've Heard It

FOR A GUY WHO HAS SPENT a good many nights of his life killing himself on stage for a laugh, my messages in these books are often dreadfully serious. And, as Samuel Goldwyn once said, "Messages are for Western Union."

I *do* apologize, but there's a time and a place for everything. And right now may be as good a time as any for a laugh.

I'll put all of this under a heading of communication because if people don't understand what we're talking about, if they don't comprehend the message we're trying to convey, we don't get very far. And then there are the messages that, while being absolutely whacko, we somehow *do* understand.

Samuel Goldwyn, who I have already quoted, and who was the G of MGM, was famous for the way he gave convoluted twists to his messages. It was Mr. Goldwyn who said: "Directors are always biting the hand that lays the golden egg." It was also he who said: "In two words: im-possible."

Other statements attributed to him include:

"We have all passed a lot of water since then."

"Gentlemen, kindly include me out."

"Anyone who goes to a psychiatrist should have his head examined."

"I had a great idea this morning, but I didn't like it."

"What we want is a story that starts with an earthquake and works its way up to a climax."

"The scene is dull. Tell him to put more life into his dying!"

"When I want your opinion, I'll give it to you!"

"It's more than magnificent, it's mediocre."

"A bachelor's life is no life for a single man."

"Why only 12 disciples? Go out and get thousands!"

Some of these are what we call malapropisms, named after Mrs. Malaprop, who knowingly or unknowingly ludicrously misused words in Sheridan's 1775 play *The Rivals*. Others are just plain strange.

Bill Peterson, who in his career coached both Florida State and the Houston Oilers, left a legacy of convoluted and ridiculously funny messages when he died in 1993 after a battle with cancer.

Said he to a team one day: "You guys pair off in groups of three, then line up in a circle."

"I got indicted into the Florida Sports Hall of Fame. They gave me a standing observation."

"I'm the football coach around here and don't you remember it!"

"You guys have to run a little more than full speed out there."

"O.K. Let's line up alphabetically by height."

My wife Kay, who is finishing up her masters in theology and family counselling, passed on *this* story. Stop me if you've heard it.

A woman went to see a marriage counsellor because she had decided that divorce was inevitable. The counsellor began the session by asking her some preliminary questions.

"Divorce," he said. "Do you have any grounds?"

"Yes, we have about an acre."

"Not quite what I mean," said the counsellor. "Do you have a grudge?"

"No, we have a carport."

Trying again, the counsellor asked: "Does he beat you up?"

"Oh, no," said the woman, "I'm always up before he is."

"Tell me," asked the now frustrated counsellor, "why do you want to divorce your husband?"

"Because when we try to talk, intelligent conversation is impossible!"

Church bulletins are often fertile ground for this kind of stuff and these, I'm told, are all legitimate.

"This afternoon there will be services in the north and south areas of the church. Children will be baptized at both ends."

"Tuesday at 3 p.m. there will be an ice cream social. All ladies giving milk, please come early."

"On Wednesday, the Ladies' Literary Society will meet. Mrs. Johnson will sing *Put me in my Little Bed,* accompanied by the pastor."

"This being Easter Sunday, we will ask Mrs. Smith to come forward to lay an egg on the altar."

"The ladies of the church have cast off clothing of every kind and they may be seen in the church basement on Friday afternoons."

"The preacher for Sunday next will be found hanging on the notice board in the porch."

In any discussion of this kind, we can't forget the fabled baseball legend Yogi Berra.

Of golf, Yogi said: "Ninety per cent of the putts that are short don't go in." Ain't it the truth?

He once said to the Yankees: "You have to give 100 per cent in the first half of the game. And if that isn't enough, in the second half you have to give what is left."

"Baseball," he said, "is 50 per cent mental and the other 90 per cent is physical."

He gave good advice. "If you come to a fork in the road, take it."

He enjoyed a good show. "I watched a Steve McQueen movie last night. He must have made it before he died."

A server once asked him if he would like his pizza cut into four or eight slices.

"Four," he said without hesitation. "I don't think I could eat eight."

He looked after himself. "I usually take a two-hour nap from one to four."

He thought things through. "Why buy luggage? You only use it when you travel."

Yogi's wife went shopping and forgot to tell him that a man was coming to fix a broken blind. The door bell rang and was answered by Yogi's son.

"Hey, dad," he hollered. "There's a man here for the Venetian blind."

"There's a couple of bucks in my pants pocket," Yogi shouted back. "Give it to him."

In his *City in Focus* newsletter, Thomas Cooper told how change was greatly affecting the life of a farmer:

"It started in '66," the farmer said, "when they changed from pounds to dollars. That doubled my overdraft. After that they changed rain to millimetres and we haven't had an inch of rain since. If that wasn't enough, they changed acres to hectares and I ended up with only half the land I once had. I decided to sell out. I put the property on the market and then they changed miles to kilometres. Now I'm too far out of town for anyone to buy the place."

An acquaintance of mine has been malaproping without letup ever since I met him. I keep a file of his stuff in my office. From all kinds of scraps of paper, napkins and coasters, I share some of his best.

On potential surgery: "I talked to a few nurses and they told me it takes at least 90 days to get the anastasia out of your system."

On his surroundings: "This room," he said, "has great ambulance."

We were up at dawn one morning and he remarked: "Great sunset!"

Newborns, he observed, "come complete with a biblical chord."

"Too many people," said he, "are incementive to others." A concrete statement if ever there was one.

He has been known to mail letters in vanilla envelopes, or alternatively, to courier them by percolator.

He once confided that Gladys Knight and the Pimps was his favourite group.

He has been known to top up his baked potato with shower cream and once excused himself by saying that he had two brains and one of them wasn't working.

Like many Canadians, he invests to defer taxes, in RSVPs.

When he travels, he takes buggage, and instance cash.

We were once privileged to meet and hear that great Second World War woman of song, who he remembered as Vera Dame Broad.

At a formal function, he asked: "Who's sitting at the headline?"

He re-named the First Nations people of upcoast British Columbia the Hyatt Indians. The Haida would be charmed.

He once called me from his car, using his nuclear phone.

Of my fund-raising efforts through golf for the Canadian Red Cross, he observed the familiar Red Cross logo flying high above the first tee and asked: "How come we're raising money for Switzerland?"

I love the guy, and to this day I have no idea whether he knows what he's saying or whether he's totally in control and just happens to be a lot funnier than the rest of us.

I just keep writing it down.

*This country was not built by
men who relied on
somebody else to take care of them.
It was built by men who
relied on themselves,
who dared to shape their own lives,
who had enough courage to
blaze new trails,
enough confidence in themselves to
take the necessary risks.*

—J. Ollié Edmunds

CHAPTER 39

All in a Day's Work

I MEET A LOT OF PEOPLE in my publishing and public speaking life. Meeting new people goes with the territory. I meet people in airports, on planes, at lunches and dinners, on golf courses and on street corners in distant cities.

Most people I meet I know I will never see again. Unfortunately, they are just faces, smiling or otherwise, in the human crowd. Sometimes, of course, I get closer. There is an exchange of conversation, of cards, and subsequent follow up. Sometimes friendships develop.

I was thinking about all of this at a pre-Christmas lunch late last year when four of us at the table were talking about our schedules and how we handle time.

"Interesting," I said, "but the question I am most often asked in my travels is what do I actually *do* on a day-to-day basis? How do I juggle things? What's important? How do I make a priority of something? What counts?"

"So what do you tell them?" I was asked.

"I tell them that no matter what you do and how much you attempt to control things, time rolls on, things happen, the challenges never stop – and it's invariably interesting."

"To me it sounds a bit *depressing*," said one.

I dug deep into my jacket and pulled out a pocket diary. I use it to record all the highlights of my days.

"Depressing?" I said. "Let's take a typical day, and you can judge for yourselves."

"You record *everything?*"

"Nope, just enough here to help me remember." I thumbed through the pages. "O.K. Let's do Monday, November 27th; as typical and perhaps untypical as any day."

"Shoot."

"I was on the road by 6 a.m., heading off from my home in the Vancouver suburbs for a breakfast meeting at the Inn at Semi-ahmoo, just over the border in Washington State. I was meeting the Snapple juice people. They invited me down to talk about the possibility of them sponsoring an event in January that would involve the Restaurant Association. I would be guest speaker."

"Uh huh."

"I'm glad I left early because it's a great drive, mostly on the freeway, but some of the way through coastal scrub and farm country, through a wildlife reserve and right by a PGA golf course that's rated among the top 25 in the world."

"No kidding!"

"The Inn is in a great setting – a cove right across from the border town of Blaine, where the tall ships used to anchor and take on lumber and fish for markets around the world."

"All this is in your *diary*?"

"No, I read about it at the Inn and I remember it. Anyway, I'm heading down the last hill toward the hotel and right at the side of the road, two deer are grazing. A couple of perfect Bambis. The sun was just coming up, there was a trace of mist, it was absolutely picture perfect. There couldn't have been a better start anywhere to a meeting, or a day."

"And the meeting?"

"My meeting with the Snapple people reminded me how you can learn a lot of fascinating stuff in the course of a business day. One piece of info came to light when one of my hosts asked me if I knew how Snapple could break into the hotel mini-bar market. I told him that I really couldn't help, and casually asked if business in the mini-bar market was a big deal? 'Big deal? Mini-bars in hotels,' he said, 'are a billion-dollar-a-year business.' I rarely have time to even *open* a mini-bar, let alone *use* one, but *someone* obviously does!

"I asked them about the Jerry Seinfeld-Snapple connection. Does he really drink it? They laughed and told me that one of Jerry's favourite drinks is Peach Snapple. One day, when the writing team was brainstorming, Jerry wrote in a casual reference to Snapple, it got a shot on the show, the drink took off and the rest is history."

"You worked out a deal?"

"Yep."

"Then?"

"When I got back to the office, Glen Ringdal, a former vice-president with the NHL Vancouver Canucks called me to see if *Pacific Golf Magazine*, one of the new members of our publishing family, would consider a sponsorship of an annual Jewish dinner. The event had a golf theme, so Glen felt *Pacific Golf* would be a natural fit. While we were talking he also asked me if I would consider sitting on the fund-raising board of Simon Fraser University."

"And . . . ?"

"I worked out a deal on the dinner and I'm considering the second offer. The end of the day was as interesting and as memorable as the beginning of the day. My partner and I sat down to dinner with our lawyers of 20 years to celebrate the successful conclusion of a lengthy litigation involving the buyout of two of the company's original shareholders. It was the end of one era for the company and the beginning of another. It was fitting that we were dining at Trader Vic's in Vancouver. After 30 fabulous years, the restaurant was closing and the space it occupied would be used in future for something else. To cap the event, our lawyers gave me a copy of the cover of the very first TV WEEK magazine. My face, as the magazine's new publisher, was superimposed into a picture of Tony Orlando and Dawn. We laughed a lot that night, and remembered a lot."

"You pick up on a lot of things . . ."

"I try to. I think that what I remembered from that night is that it always makes sound economic sense to hire the best people. Hire the best lawyers and the best accountants – the cost of their services will come back to you a hundred times over."

"Quite a day," said one of the guys at the table. "From deer at dawn to Tony Orlando and Dawn."

"Whatever happened to those guys?" I said. "*Man*, that's a long time ago."

You are the same today as
you will be in
five years from now
except for two things —
The books you read and the
people you meet.
—Charlie "T" Jones

CHAPTER 40

On the Run

AT THE OFFICE, I MAKE ABOUT 50 phone calls a day, answer that
many more – solicited and unsolicited – talk to accountants and
lawyers, to the company's senior management, to heads of
departments, editors, art directors and to others inside and outside of the company. I read two or three local and out-of-town
newspapers and magazines, at home and in the office, and scan
the company's own magazines before and after they are published. As a commuter, I spend morning and evening time on the
road. As I drive, I make and receive cellular calls from any number of people, listen to tapes, and catch the occasional newscast
to keep in touch.

In the times between, I travel extensively on company business and pursue my second career as a public speaker. I keep in
close touch while I'm at home and away with my wife and fami-

ly; I volunteer my services to several organizations; I keep my eyes open for business and other opportunities; and I try to have some fun along the way – smelling the roses and putting the greens, adding balance to my business life.

Sometimes this life of mine gets talked about when I meet people in the course of my travels. Some of them say that life is too short to keep up this kind of pace, and I don't argue with them. All I say is that long hours and a hectic pace come with the kind of life I choose to lead, and longer hours and a more hectic pace may be necessary if they're looking for something more in *their* lives. I tell them that, despite the fullness of my schedule, I'm able to *manage* what I do, I'm able to make decisions about what my priorities will be. This is most important and I know it's a big challenge for many people to be able to take charge of their own lives.

Continuing on the theme of the previous chapter, I've picked out some more dates from my 1995 diary to share with you. I hope these notes will support what I'm saying. I just think that life can be exciting indeed.

Sunday, Oct. 1

I came back from Winston-Salem, North Carolina, to British Columbia with United Airlines after playing in the Vantage Invitational Golf Championship at Tanglewood. This was my fourth excursion to this beautiful part of the United States and, in 1995, we were defending champions in the pro am tournament. This time, we drew Ray Floyd, one of the most accomplished golfers in the seniors tour. Poor Ray. We didn't help his game at all and, no, we didn't win.

Monday, Oct. 2

I met, as I always do on Monday mornings, with all of the senior managers at Canada Wide. This ritual has continued for almost 10 years at the company. Our production manager, Corinne Smith, is in charge of these meetings and they are focused, well planned and have a precise purpose. We achieve what we set out to achieve. I believe in agendas. They are absolutely essential.

I had lunch with Joe Segal at Chartwell, a great restaurant in Vancouver's Four Seasons Hotel. Every time I go there, I'm reminded of a trip to England that I took years ago when we paid a visit to the original Chartwell, the home of Sir Winston Churchill and after which the restaurant was named. What I remember most vividly from that visit was a wall that Sir Winston had built when he was a member of the bricklayer's union. What an amazing man. As well as everything else, during his "wilderness years" he learned how to lay bricks!

I was looking forward to my lunch with Joe. He is a prominent Canadian businessman and, along with all kinds of other public service activities, he is chancellor of British Columbia's Simon Fraser University. I admire him tremendously.

Joe and I have been business associates for many years. Clearly, he has made a substantial fortune from his endeavours and I have always felt blessed on the occasions we've shared lunch. Joe's table at Chartwell was ready for his arrival at precisely 12:15 p.m. He is always on time. So was I, and for the next hour or so I was ready to take mental notes and learn from one of the best in the business. Joe was candid at lunch, sharing stories of his highs and lows, offering thoughts as to how he might have done things differently given a second chance. I listened spellbound.

As lunch ended he confirmed that, yes, he and wife Rosalie would be happy to assist in one of my upcoming endeavours. The Canadian Red Cross had just appointed me Centennial Ambassador for 1996. In March, the Canadian Red Cross would be 100 years old.

As part of a larger program, I had arranged for the Countess of Mountbatten, daughter of the late Earl Mountbatten of Burma to be a special guest of honour for the celebration. Joe and Rosalie would open their beautiful Vancouver home for a private reception during the Countess's visit and pick up the entire tab for the evening. I finished the lunch by accepting Joe's challenge to use the event to raise $100,000 for the Red Cross!

That night, I entertained a number of clients in the Canada Wide suite at Vancouver's GM Place. The Vancouver Canucks played the Calgary Flames. I can't remember who won.

Wednesday, Oct. 4
The BCPGA annual golf pro am is being held at the Vancouver Golf & Country Club. *Pacific Golf*, one of our magazines, is a sponsor and the shotgun start is scheduled for 8 a.m. I'm there to play, but again I'm out of the money.

My mind is on the Astra Awards taking place tonight. I'm to be recognized by the food industry in Western Canada along with my good friend Brandt Louie, who is president of H.Y. Louie Co. Ltd., a major player in the Western Canada food industry. Nearly 1,000 people are paying $100 each for the evening's salute. Phew!

Having put on many dinners at the Hyatt Regency Hotel, I am comforted by the fact that the 1,001 details that have to be looked after for an event like this are being looked after this time by someone else.

My speech of thanks followed some glowing words from longtime mentor and former employer Mel Cooper. Good old Mel. He's a man I will always admire.

I said no one is a success unless a lot of other people want you to be a success. I said awards like this don't come easily or overnight. It took 30 years – from my early days in the food industry delivering flyer proofs to Canada Safeway and other major chains, to links that followed through our publishing of industry magazines, to other programs that came about because I saw opportunity. I was honoured to have been chosen for the award. It was a magical night that I will always remember.

Thursday, Oct. 5

Today we concluded the purchase of *Equity*, the only real competition that our magazine, *BC Business,* has ever had. *BC Business* Magazine, acquired from Vancouver businessman Jim Pattison about five years ago, has been slogging it out with *Equity* for 12 long, tough years and this afternoon I will meet the entire *Equity* staff and invite them all to join the Canada Wide team. I think this purchase blew the minds of a lot of publishing observers in British Columbia. I suspect many thought for the longest time that the deal would go the other way. We surprised them all.

It's now 6:15 p.m. and I'm waiting to board Air Canada's evening flight to Winnipeg, then to drive for two hours to Brandon to address the Credit Unions of Manitoba. The flight arrives late so I decide to stay in Winnipeg and drive to Brandon in the morning. I slept like a log.

Friday, Oct. 6

I drove to Brandon as scheduled. I don't care how much people malign the landscape of the Canadian Prairies, I love it out there. Big country, big sky and, as they say, no mountains to block the view. I conducted a three-hour seminar, using my 25 success secrets as a basis for the presentation. Some 300 delegates and a great crowd. I sold and signed a number of my books before driving back to Winnipeg to fly home.

Sunday, Oct. 8

Once every two years I get a chance to speak at my own church, Calvary Christian in Surrey, British Columbia. Two services, and both of them sold out! I donated 200 books for the congregation to buy. All of the money raised would be donated back to the church for special projects. Spent almost an hour signing books for the congregation and thoroughly enjoyed the experience. Family dinner at 4 p.m.

Wednesday, Oct. 11

As a former winner of the Entrepreneur of the Year Award, I was invited to breakfast with Canadian Prime Minister Jean Chretien in the Crystal Room of the Metropolitan Hotel in Vancouver. He spoke of the importance of the entrepreneurial spirit in a growing Canada. I believe in that spirit.

The Entrepreneurs Association credo?

"I do not choose to be a common man. It is my right to be uncommon, if I can. I seek opportunity, not security! I do not wish to be a kept citizen, humbled and dulled by having the state look after me. I want to take the calculated risk, to dream and to build, to fail and to succeed. I refuse to barter incentive for a dole, I prefer the challenges of life to the guaranteed existence; the thrill of fulfilment to the state calm of Utopia. I will not trade freedom for beneficence, nor my dignity for a handout. I will NEVER cower before any master, nor bend to any threat. It is my heritage to stand erect, proud and unafraid; to think and act for myself, to enjoy the benefit of my creations and to face the world boldly and say, 'This, with God's help, I have done.' All this is what it means to be an entrepreneur."

Friday, Oct. 13

I addressed the Prince George Chamber of Commerce in central British Columbia. A sold-out audience. Spent almost an hour signing books. I was invited back to the annual general meeting in March 1996. Must make a note.

Monday, Oct. 16

At 8 a.m. I spoke to 350 men and women from the Investor's Group. My theme centred on the importance of living every day to the fullest.

At 7 p.m., I was at the BCPGA Awards Banquet at the brand-new $165 million General Motors Place in downtown Vancouver. What a great building this is! At the banquet I was named Patron of the Year, recognizing the birth of *Pacific Golf Magazine* and its contribution to golf in British Columbia. Sales Manager Stephen Thomas, Editor Bonnie Irving and Art Director Gavin Orpen really deserve the credit and I'm glad they were there.

I should have stayed longer, but I had to catch the last flight to Calgary so I could get to Edmonton the next morning to address almost 1,000 realtors from across the country at a meeting of the Canadian Real Estate Association. There was a ton of energy in that audience. They gave me two standing ovations and I spent two hours signing books and talking to dozens of wonderful sales professionals from across Canada. I was delayed in my return to Vancouver, which meant I was unable to introduce Brian Tracy, part of the Peak Performers presentations that we co-sponsor at the Vancouver Trade and Convention Centre. Sorry about that, Brian. I know you knocked 'em dead!

Tuesday, Oct. 17

I had lunch at the Vancouver Club with Vancouver businessman David Bentall. You may remember him from Chapter 26 in this book – the guy who won't buy an ad! I invited David to join my committee for the Red Cross 100th anniversary reception at Joe and Rosalie Segal's home. (Remember the $100,000 challenge!) David said yes, without hesitation. He, too, had an agenda. His personal project is Pearson College of the Pacific on Vancouver Island and could I help *him?* We agreed to host a lunch as part of *BC Business* magazine's major event of the year, the Top 100. He would provide former United States president Jimmy Carter as a speaker. These lunches get better and better. Must exercise!

Monday, Oct. 23

I addressed the National Real Estate Service sales group at 8 a.m., then made a mad dash to Vancouver International to catch a flight to Calgary where we had been invited to make a presentation to win the contract to publish the Canadian Airlines in-flight magazine. I wonder if not getting the contract had anything to do with the fact that we could only fly Air Canada to make it to the meeting on time! I never get really disappointed if we are unable to make a deal. There will always be another opportunity, another magazine, another project. It's best not to get hung up on things. That's when costly mistakes are made. Feel free to walk away from any deal unless it's life threatening. Most aren't.

Wednesday, Oct. 25

I caught a 7 a.m. flight to Penticton in the interior of British Columbia to have breakfast with Captain Jack Boddington, chairman of the Royal Life Saving Society. Jack was instrumental in naming me Governor for B.C. and the Yukon of this splendid organization. Her Majesty the Queen is the worldwide patron.

I had the opportunity to be master of ceremonies at the society's Bravery and Rescue Awards ceremony a few months earlier, taking Jack's place when he was recovering from heart surgery. He will be there next time to join the B.C. lieutenant governor and me when we present awards for bravery to another group of deserving human beings who have unselfishly risked their lives to save the life of someone else.

From Penticton, I drove north through the Okanagan Valley to the Vernon Golf & Country Club. I spoke to 250 people from a variety of businesses who, with others across the province, are celebrating small business week. Then back over my tracks to Kelowna to make the same presentation to a different audience at the Capri Hotel. I ended both speeches with a strong and supportive reference to the people in our business. I said that many of our *own* dreams can only be accomplished when we inspire *others* to greatness. I quoted a Chinese proverb that says if you want a year of prosperity, grow grain; if you want 10 years of prosperity, grow trees; if you want a hundred years of prosperity, grow people.

Friday, Oct. 27

Another small business awards week banquet. More than 300 people crowd into the Holiday Inn at Chilliwack in the Fraser Valley and I go to work on them. I know it's the end of the week, but I like speaking on Friday nights. People are up and ready to party, or, in this case, to listen. My topic is How to Soar with the Eagles, the title of my first book, and a topic I love. Each member of the audience received a book as part of the program and long into the night I sign them. A satisfying end to the week.

Saturday, Oct. 28

Canadian Airlines International flight #956 takes me to Edmonton to address the Western Educators Conference – some 250 teachers and others from across Alberta. These are the people who are planting the seeds of dreams into the lives of thousands of young people who will shape the next generation. It's an important audience. Using the letters in the word dreams, I shared some thoughts. D stood for dare, R for risk, E for excellence, A for attitude, M for mission and S for success. I think they all apply to people who teach.

At 4:30, I left for Toronto and dinner with Stan Smith, a close friend and vice-president of sales for RJR Macdonald Inc., Canada, at the Four Seasons Hotel, my favourite. On each visit to the hotel I learn something new about customer service. Unobtrusive and elusive for anyone who is trying to copy it. But memorable. Excellence in service is something that must be done with honesty and sincerity to work the way it does. How are the messages passed on? I would love to sit in on a training session and learn their secrets.

Our chief want is someone who will
make us what we know
we can become
—Ralph Waldo Emerson

CHAPTER 41

My Dream, Courtesy of Mr. Sandman

THERE ARE MOMENTS IN OUR LIVES that we remember better than others because they trigger mechanisms within us that set us off in new life directions. The *right* directions. The way we're supposed to be going.

These triggers are sometimes delayed. We know that lifetime hobbies we thoroughly enjoyed for years and years really *should* have been more than hobbies. We built fine furniture or planted gardens or tinkered with cars on weekends and loved what we did, and Monday to Friday we slogged it out in the trenches in a job that drove us crazy. Not enough courage to quit? Not enough courage to surrender the *security* that came with the job? Who knows?

I have two careers. One of them as president of a publishing company and the other as a public speaker. I enjoy both careers, but if I may share a secret just with you, I will tell you that it is the roar of the greasepaint and the smell of the crowd that more often fulfils my fondest dreams.

Being president of a publishing company and having an outstanding team of people to help make it a success makes it possible for public speaking to be much more than just a hobby. I'm into it big time!

Let me tell you about the "trigger" that pushed *me* onto the wicked stage.

When I was nine, we lived in Greenford in Middlesex, England. Between movies every Saturday morning at the local cinema, the Granada Theatre, there was a show for kids and everyone came. The brave ones in the audience were encouraged to get up on the stage and do a "thing." I sang *Mr. Sandman, Send Me a Dream,* and I clearly remember knocking 'em dead.

The warm applause that came back from all those little British kids turned something on inside me that morning and while my stage career didn't immediately continue, I knew that whatever had happened at the Granada felt very good indeed, and some day I would make it happen again.

Along the way, as a sideline to "real" work, I made an additional living as a standup comedian, as a speaker before and after dinner, always stretching myself on the stage.

About 15 years ago, when the publishing company was beginning to make its first significant mark in Canada, I began my second serious career as a man with a message. In an ever-widening circle of audiences that would, in due course, reach out to points as distant and diversified as London and Hong Kong, I began to share my life philosophy, to tell stories, to attempt to motivate the desire for success in others.

Today I speak to groups as small as 25 in tiny rooms, to crowds of 3,000 in the largest of auditoriums. I travel about 100,000 miles every year, and while, from time to time, I get terribly tired of airports, hotels, cab drivers and atrocious sound systems, the rush that comes with every presentation never ceases. I cannot believe how lucky I am to be compensated so handsomely for a craft I love so dearly.

I learned at the outset that public speaking is not a profession for wimps. It requires endless preparation to remain topical, and tons of practice to be more than interesting. You can never fake it.

I remember reading a book on the art of preaching by one John Scott in which he told the story of a lazy Anglican minister who had long ago given up preparing sermons. He had considerable intelligence and fluency of speech and figured these talents were enough to inspire the flock each Sunday morning. He was so convinced that his program was right that he solemnly vowed to preach extemporaneously for the rest of his life. Not only no notes, but no nothing!

It all worked reasonably well until one day, a few minutes before the morning service, who should walk in but the bishop. The minister got a bit nervous. He could bluff the congregation, but could he fake it with the bishop? So the minister told the bishop of his vow, and the bishop nodded his head and settled into a pew to await the morning service.

Halfway through the sermon, to the minister's great consternation, the bishop rose, walked to the back of the church, scribbled a note, and left it on the vestry table. Confident that the note was a blessing of his words, the minister picked it up at the end of the service and read: "I absolve you of your vow."

I began my speaking career by accepting any and all engagements for free. I needed exposure, I needed self-confidence, I needed to hone my messages. To practise, practise, practise.

At the beginning, I was amazed at how difficult it was. There were good times and there were awful times. Messages that failed to inspire. Killer jokes that fell flat. Audiences that I under- or over-estimated. I have told the story many times about how most people would rather die than stand up and make a speech. Does this mean that these people would rather be in a casket at a funeral than up front presenting the eulogy?

Regardless of the ups and downs of the trade, I always felt the same energy that I had felt at the Granada Theatre. And 500 presentations later, I gladly accepted a $100 fee to speak at a company sales meeting. I was on my professional way.

Later, as my reputation and the number of engagements increased, I joined the National Speakers Association, a Phoenix-based organization with worldwide connections. I was told that my career would move much faster with the NSA and, if I proved myself over time, I may be able to earn the designation of Certified Speaking Professional. Of the 4,000 or so NSA members, only about 225 are CSPs. I am unbelievably proud to be one of those people.

Once you have become a CSP, it is generally much easier to be booked as a speaker, the assignments are better, the rewards are greater. But the learning and the testing never stops. You're only as good as your last assignment, as the assessments that come, and are needed, from our peers and our audiences.

I have some marvellous mentors and role models, people who motivate and encourage me to get better and better. Among them, Nido Quibin, Brian Tracy, Jim Cartcart, Vanna Novak and Max Dixon are very special.

Special, too, are the agents, the hard-working people who make the bookings, work with the meeting planners, provide honest feedback on performance. My two original agents were Linda Davidson and Perry Goldsmith from Vancouver. Dottie Walters and Michelle Lemmons from Los Angeles and Dallas are among others in great agency roles.

In the fall of 1995, I had the good fortune to meet one of Canada's foremost agents for speakers. She is a dynamo with a personality so infectious it is impossible not to jump right out of your socks for her. Carol Brickenden heads up the Brickenden Group in Toronto. She heard about me through my marketing manager Jane Atkinson and asked me to speak at her annual retreat in early December.

It being a showcase presentation – a number of us were being sized up for possible future engagements – there would be no fee, and we would be responsible for our own travel costs to Toronto. Carol arranged for about 250 CEOs to come and hear 22 speakers go their best licks, a public speaking sales pitch, for want of a better description. We would be rated. I had the rare honour of being wrap-up speaker – a big risk, but bigger potential reward.

Having told Carol that I would accept her invitation, she sent me her guidelines for "punching out your passion." In it, she articulated in the best way I have ever seen something like this done, 11 fundamentals for maximizing the impact of a keynote speech. She challenged me to score a 10 with my audience for every point she had listed.

With Carol's permission, I offer a summary of her passion punching points. They may be useful to you as a speaker, as a potential speaker, as a business person.

The keynote speaker, she says, should be able to produce such an emotional connection with the audience that people rise to their feet and cheer. A standing ovation should really be the goal, to connect on an emotional level, to touch their hearts as well as their minds. To do it in 45 minutes.

Audiences want an emotional, inspirational blast that will rock them out of their seats. Frequently, the most successful way to do this is through humour. Keynote speakers must have a comedic bent. Humour is a very serious business. Either you've got it or you haven't. If the keynote speaker is not strong with this presentation style, then being dynamic and having a poignancy and power in delivery works too. Either way, the speaker touches the audience's emotions, hearts and minds.

Keynote speakers have generally "arrived," experience and credibility-wise. They've become experts in their field. Perhaps they've written a book or two – even better if it's a best-seller.

He or she has a responsibility to deliver a relevant message in keeping with the theme, providing the emotional punch to launch the day.

The 11 key characteristics of a top-notch keynote speaker?

- Passion. First and foremost a special something that puts a glow around you. A conviction about the subject that is supported by experience and is quickly obvious by the energy and enthusiasm of the presenter.
- Exceptional story-telling ability. An absolute must!
- Confidence on the platform.
- Obvious and believable leadership in your given field.
- The ability to speak extemporaneously. Little reference to notes except as A/V aids. (But remember the story of the parson. You don't just make it all up!)
- Humour. A wonderful conduit for connecting with and inspiring the audience.
- Commitment to keep learning and passing along client experiences on an on-going basis. There's nothing as revealing about a speaker as stale material!
- Respect for the audience. Humility laced with a strong dose of confidence is a powerful blend.
- Courtesy – off the stage. As important as platform skills.
- Having the courage to try new things with existing and new material and presentation style. Willingness to be self-revealing.
- Grace. This quality, or lack of it, has a lot to do with how long a speaker lasts in the business.

Carol told me that Canada is developing a strong network of internationally successful speakers who are excelling in the tough, competitive keynote world. But to nourish the keynote material, the most highly regarded presenters continue to take on real, live consulting and training assignments. They never stop doing their homework and remain as "working professionals." She says it is absolutely key to their success and credibility that they continue to speak in the first person from their own experience and perspective. (Yes, I intend to also keep my day job!)

I don't know what *you* think, but I was most grateful to receive Ms. Brickenden's public speaking pointers and I will always keep them close at hand.

I used the outline to prepare for my presentation to her chosen audience at Toronto's delightful Old Mill and, with what I trust is grace, I can report that Carol's written assessment of my performance left me walking on air right through the Christmas holidays. And for that, I am particularly grateful.

It seems like a long time ago that I stood on that stage in Greenford and sang my heart out to Mr. Sandman. But on reflection, I guess he listened.

And with a great deal of happiness and satisfaction, with commitment and with every-time-out passion, I continue to live a dream that magically came true.

CHAPTER 42

Begin the Dream

I HAVE WRITTEN ELSEWHERE of my beginnings with Variety Club International. Thirty years ago, I was called from a Vancouver nightclub stage to add my talents to a cause for special children. I willingly accepted and today Variety and its fund-raising programs remain high on my personal list of priorities. It's a wonderful organization and its high-profile activities have been tremendously beneficial to the lives of thousands of children around the world.

While the drive for funds never stops, in British Columbia the biggest fund-raising event of the year is the Variety Club Show of Hearts, a telethon that is broadcast throughout the province by British Columbia Television on the weekend closest to Valentine's Day. It's a spectacular show that attracts the best in the business and a huge studio and television audience that consistently shows just how generous people can be for a cause that can directly help others.

I have been involved in the telethon stage for many years. Along with the rest of the telethon family, I get swept up in the spirit of the venture and delight each year in seeing the final total up in lights – a salute to thousands and thousands of caring people.

In 1996, the telethon was to reach the great age of 30. It would look back on nearly 700 television hours that were supported by more than 150,000 volunteers, and more than 25,000 performers.

There is one more significant statistic. During the course of its 30 years, the telethon has raised more than $57,000,000 for Variety's special kids!

In 1995, I was honoured when the telethon chose as its theme the thrust behind my then most-recent book, *You Can if You Believe You Can.*

Later in the year, as we began to plan for 1996, I was delighted when the title for *this* book became the theme for the telethon that would soon be unfolding its 30th anniversary banner.

As a member of the organizing committee, I suppose that I *do* have more than usual input into the direction that the telethon will go. But regardless of how the decision was made, I earnestly believe that big things really do begin with dreams of all sizes.

President John F. Kennedy challenged America to meet a deadline and put a man on the moon. It began with a dream and it ended as "one giant leap for mankind."

The American poet Carl Sandburg wrote: "Nothing happens unless first a dream." He was right. We can stumble around in darkness, but it's our dreams that bring in the light. Dreams challenge, dreams present opportunity.

Variety Club's telethon began all those years ago with a dream and each year we get together in committee and dream again. You don't raise $57,000,000 in 30 years without doing a whole heap of dreaming. You don't help a special kid without dreaming that something better can happen for him – and doing something about it.

You can *feel* it when people begin to dream big dreams. Their eyes brighten, they smile and, if you look hard enough, you can detect halos around their heads. You just *know* they're onto something and nothing can stop them.

For the dreamers, there's no pessimism, no looking back. The bridge will be built. The idea will work. The goal will be achieved. The sky, and beyond, is there for the reaching.

I will always be a dreamer. Some of my dreams will be small dreams, and others, for as long as I live, will be dreams of *awesome* proportion.

When it was decided that the telethon of 1996 would be themed around *It Begins with a Dream*, Vancouver lyricist and telethon producer Shel Piercy wrote the words and Bill Sample wrote the music for a song that would open the show. It's a beautiful song, and in its telethon setting, I have every confidence that it will be a major factor in helping the telethon achieve its objective.

These are Shel Piercy's words, which I use with his permission.

I believe in Santa Claus,
I believe in magic wands,
Talking frogs,
Singing bears,
The magic in the land of Oz,
Over the rainbow . . .

I believe in starry nights,
I believe in holding tight,
Sharing tears,
Sharing joy,
Loving arms can make it right . . .
Don't ever let me go . . .
I believe that kisses heal,
I believe that love is real,
Begin with one,
Begin with two,
You know it works, it's up to you.

And I believe,
And I believe,
And I believe . . .

It begins with a dream . . .

It begins with a dream,
No matter how hard,
No matter how high,
No matter the what,
The where or the why,
Whether climbing a mountain,
Or writing a book,
Finding a new friend,
It's there if you look,
It begins with a dream,
For you and for me,
It begins with a dream.

Love is like a newborn's dreams,
Full of hope, no in between,
Live the hope,
And dream the dream,
Your life begins when dreams are seen,
And I believe,
And I believe,
Do you believe . . .

It begins with a dream . . .

It begins with a dream,
No matter how hard,
No matter how high,

No matter the what,
The where or the why,
Whether climbing a mountain,
Or writing a book,
Finding a new friend,
It's there if you look,
It begins with a dream,
For you and for me,
It begins with a dream.

It may sound too trite, or too simple,
Too easy you feel,
You have to believe us,
Cuz dreams will come true,
Just by wishing them so,
Your faith is the power,
And love makes it grow!

Do you believe?
Do you believe?
Do you believe?

It begins with a dream,
No matter how hard,
No matter how high,
No matter the what,
The where or the why . . .

Whether climbing a mountain,
Or writing a book,
Finding a new friend,
It's there if you look,
It begins with a dream,
It begins with a dream,
It begins with a dream,
It begins with a dream,
It begins with a dream,
It begins with a dream,
For you and for me . . .
It begins with a dream,
It begins with a dream!

Dream. And begin!

Dream and Begin
with
Peter Legge Live!

The dream of this book, its stories and its inspirational content can come alive for you in a powerful and exciting way. Peter Legge can highlight your conference, seminar or sales meeting with a dynamic, energy-charged keynote address.

For inquiries about engagements, books, tapes or videos:
- Phone (604) 299-7311 or Fax (604) 299-9188
- e-mail Address: plegge@canadawide.com
- Write: Peter Legge Management Co. Ltd.
4th Floor, 4180 Lougheed Hwy.
Burnaby, British Columbia
Canada V5C 6A7.